CRIME

Changing Society and the Churches

Crime

T. J. Gorringe

First published in Great Britain in 2004 by
Society for Promoting Christian Knowledge
Holy Trinity Church
Marylebone Road
London NW1 4DU

British Library Cataloguing-in-Publication Data
A catalogue record for this book is available from the British Library

ISBN 0-281-05652-8

10 9 8 7 6 5 4 3 2 1

Designed and typeset by Kenneth Burnley, Wirral, Cheshire
Printed in Malta by Gutenberg Press Limited

The mood and temper of the public in regard to the treatment of crime and criminals is one of the most unfailing tests of the civilisation of any country.

Winston Churchill

Contents

Changing Society and the Churches

The social teaching of the churches from 1900 to 1970 came either from members of small radical Christian groups or else from the perspective of the established order of society. Today, neither approach will work. Small left-wing groups flourished in inner urban areas and provided support to the poor up to the 1970s. Much of Christian socialism was spread through groups that may have been small nationally but which were of immense importance locally. Campaigning groups still exist but the crucial difference is that they generally do not have any religious commitment. They are instead quite secular bodies in which some members of faith communities are deeply involved.

Equally the middle axiom approach of the churches (where the accepted wisdom of social experts was put alongside the wisdom of leaders of the Church) does not work either. The churches are too marginal to bring about this influence on society, although a few examples of this reasoning remain in the main denominations. But it is not a model for doing Christian social ethics overall any more. The alliance of secular wisdom and liberal theology has largely collapsed as well.

However, there is still an enormous need to change society, and the Church must be challenged to think about how this can be done. Hence the title of this series is Changing Society and the Churches. The series incorporates authors who can address this need. Their arguments might not necessarily come from any one political or religious viewpoint: this is not a left-wing or a right-wing series. Rather, it includes authors who can speak to the secular world using arguments that resonate in modern society, yet employ theological resources and the Christian heritage of spirituality to support their claims. It is equally important that these arguments are designed to change society and to get Christians involved.

Can such a thing be done? We would point to the example of Rowan Williams as an author who has long resonated with society and understands contemporary culture, and yet is not afraid to use examples from theology, spirituality and Christian engagement in society to back up his arguments. The result is a language that is neither 'churchy' nor secular and watered down. It is realistic about how marginal the churches are but is not pessimistic. It speaks of the need for social change and is prepared to form alliances with non-Christian groups, but without denying the Christian basis of the argument.

The books in the series have a concrete reference and are aware that these issues demand action without offering facile solutions. They are books that explore new possibilities for society, whether from a right-wing or a left-wing position. All the books suggest why change is desirable and how it is possible.

The series is international in scope, although its concreteness may well draw on English examples, at least in the first books, since we wish authors to draw on their experience and our first authors are English. Later books may well argue from a viewpoint other than an English one. Increasingly both theology and the experience of Christians can no longer be confined to one country, and the challenges of the twenty-first century are expressed across different cultures and societies. That may well mean offering a different understanding of the relationship of society and Church for the British situation. Even so, it is important that wherever the author comes from there is an engagement with secular society using the resources of Christian tradition and theology. The aim is to bring about social change and church involvement.

This book on crime by Tim Gorringe discusses the nature of crime in an advanced industrial society. He points out that much crime is committed as fraud and those who commit crimes such as burglary come from deeply alienated strata of society. The book is excellent in relating theology, criminology and social theory in a way that enables the possibility of a constructive approach to crime and the restoration of a community based on peace and justice. This is a powerful book that will make a much needed contribution to the debate on the future of criminal justice and which draws deeply on Christian tradition.

Al McFadyen
Department of Theology and Religious Studies, University of Leeds

Peter Sedgwick
Board for Social Responsibility, Church of England

1 | **Shalom**

Theology and criminal justice

The most cursory survey of the Scriptures of the Church makes clear that the connection between Christian theology and the themes of sin and crime is anything but factitious. The Old and New Testaments are full of stories of crime and punishment, often of the most horrendous kind, which would more than satisfy the appetite of any tabloid for sex and violence. The texts include many detailed laws relating both to crimes against the person and property crime, and in Deuteronomy there is early reflection on the role of the state in all this. God is depicted as giving the law from Sinai; Jesus endorses this law, and it is one of the central foci of Paul's letters, some of which are written from prison. All the paraphernalia of criminal justice – courts, prisons, guards, secondary punishments – are familiar aspects of the narrative. Above all, the whole Christian story is organized around a story of judicial execution. And Jesus is crucified, as Luke puts it, 'the criminals with him'.

Law plays an equally large part in the history of the Church. The Christian emperor Justinian codified Roman law in 529, describing it as the exercise of his Christian duty, and the digests of this which survived were the basis of the rediscovery and reapplication of Roman law in Europe after the tenth century. Throughout the Middle Ages some of the most famous and able monks, including at least one Archbishop of Canterbury, Lanfranc, were jurists, and clergy and theologians acted as judges and lawyers and made profound innovations in jurisprudence. In England a bishop served as Lord Chancellor as late as the end of the seventeenth century. Thomas Aquinas recast what he had learned from both patristic and Greek sources in depicting a hierarchy of eternal, natural and human law and established a tradition of jurisprudence which has distinguished followers to this day. Throughout this period canon law regulated not only ecclesiastical affairs but also matters of sexual morality. On some accounts the Church was implicated in the decline of tort, civil law, and the rise of criminal law. The Inquisitor became the public prosecutor; the heretic became the subhuman criminal; heresy became deviance and eventually 'crime'. The criminal justice system, some argue, is fundamentally a form of secularized Inquisition (Bianchi, 1994). Luther began his Reformation with a bonfire of canon law. 'Jurists are bad Christians,' he declared. 'Of the Gospel jurists know nothing, therefore they are rightly excluded from the circuit of divinity.' But so tightly were law and theology bound together in Christian Europe that Lutheran and Reformed found themselves producing commentaries on the law and a Christian jurisprudence. Within two decades of the start of the Reformation magistrates were depicted as the custodians of the Decalogue, princes as the true bishops of the Church. The Church was present in court in the person of the preacher of the Assize sermon, while judges were urged to pray and submit themselves to Scripture before making their judgements. This position was defined antagonistically over against the Anabaptists who, appealing to the New Testament, denied the right of Christians to go to court or to bear the sword. The struggle between these two groups was the bitterest in Protestantism.

The intimate connection between Church and law, characteristic of Christendom, found expression not only in the continuance of bishops in the law-making body of the House of Lords, in Britain, but even more significantly in the appointment of parsons as magistrates. At the moment when that connection began to come loose, the earnest Baptist John Howard began a movement for prison reform which spread throughout Europe, a task later continued by Quakers like Elizabeth Fry. Following their lead, Christian socialists pleaded for a new understanding of crime. At the end of the twentieth century Mennonite theologians, in particular, once again challenged Christian understandings of both law and crime, and some legal theorists looked to this work to understand possible ways forward in policy. Law and crime have never been a side issue in the Church.

During the period of the Church's ascendancy theology and Church bore on criminal justice through influencing and helping to construct structures of affect. By these are meant the lived understanding which underpins any society above the level of pure anarchy. Although for much of the period of Christendom it was actually churchmen who made the laws, and who acted as judges, the mutual impact of Church and criminal justice has to be understood more subtly than simply in terms of direct borrowing in either direction. The idea of structures of affect allows us to do that and a document like the Anglican Book of Common Prayer is a fascinating case of a text which conveys profound social and penal ideas in an oblique way. Without doubt it influenced ideas of criminal justice in England, above all in the eighteenth and early nineteenth centuries. But that is 'then'. What about the present, when, in Britain, a mere 4 per cent of the population any longer 'go to church'? Is theological reflection and church action an irrelevance in a secular society? It is important in this matter for Christians not to delude themselves on this question, to romanticize or dream about re-creating Christendom, to take comfort from the idea that the majority continue to believe even if they no longer belong. The theologian will want to put sharp questions to the nature of this believing. At the same time, and especially in this area, there are reasons for thinking that Christian contributions to aspects of general social concern remain important. They are important to the degree that they speak truthfully of the human condition as people find it, and show that they enable practical and healing interventions. The question of how we understand the human condition is perhaps the most fundamental area in which theology has affected our understanding of criminal justice.

Two visions of social order

Tacit answers to the questions of the kind of society we have or want, and the deeper question of what it means to be human, underlie every aspect of the debate about criminal justice. Crime, law and punishment constitute no autonomous realm, a contention illustrated by the fact that what is understood by each of these terms varies markedly from society to society, even in the contemporary world. It follows that to address issues in crime is to address issues in society. Since, as we have seen, Scripture and church tradition have profoundly shaped answers to such questions theology does not come as an outsider to the debate but as an essential partner.

In the Western tradition there are, broadly speaking, two responses to these questions. On the one hand there is the response, for which the most famous spokesman is Hobbes, that humans are wolves which prey on one another. Primitive society is the 'war of all against all' and law is essential to keep these aggressive instincts in check. Such a view was perfectly expressed by the eighteenth-century legal reformer Beccaria, according to whom,

> The purpose of law is to serve the common good. Laws are conditions under which men, naturally independent, united themselves in society. Weary of living in a continual state of war, and of enjoying a liberty which became of little value, from the uncertainty of its duration, they sacrificed one part of it, to enjoy the rest in peace and security.

This account had a deep resonance in the Christian tradition, one strand of which believed, in the words of the fifth response of the Heidelberg catechism, that 'man is inclined by nature to hate both God and his neighbour'. Predatory crimes are to be expected. Retributivism, the theory that offending must be punished for the moral order to be maintained, was consonant with this view. A dark, even tragic, view of society is presupposed, classically expressed in Augustine's *City of God*. Here we have no lasting city and God's kingdom will never be realized here on earth. Rulers and law-makers are essential to keep order. We do not, like Kant, deify the moral law and believe that the execution of 'the last murderer' would be necessary for its validity not to be impugned but, given the realities of human nature, we recognize the tragic necessity of the operations of criminal justice. Writing not long after the end of World War II Karl Barth noted that it was precisely in view of the Christian community's knowledge of the kingdom and the grace of God that,

> It knows how dangerous man is and how endangered by himself. It knows him as a sinner, that is as a being who is always on the point of opening the sluices through which, if he were not checked in time, chaos and nothingness would break in and bring human time to an end. (Barth, 1954, p. 20)

The most famous proponent of the alternative view is Rousseau. In this view, in primitive society all is peace. No unnatural bonds are put on human instincts. Only with the introduction of property does there arise faction, hierarchy, class division and crime. Left to themselves humans are as likely to be altruistic as not. Law is an expression of alienation and the introduction of a more just society, in which the divisions of property were less marked, would see a drastic reduction in crime. This view, too, had profound theological resonance for it has always seemed to some, and not just Pelagians, that the thesis of 'total depravity' is a slander on creation. God saw all that God had created, and behold it was very good. To be sure, humankind is expelled from Eden. There is a 'fall'. But God's creation is not thereby spoiled. Grace presupposes nature – it does not destroy it, as Aquinas put it. To posit a propensity to crime as intrinsic to human nature smacks of the Manichaean heresy. Furthermore, Paul's view of the law is dialectical, and it is true that it is in part alienating but, as John Locke puts it, the primary purpose of law is not to abolish or restrain but to preserve and enlarge freedom. Again, if law is alienating, the Church exists to overcome this alienation. Paul deals with offenders by punishing them with a view to their later reintegration into the community. The priority of forgiveness puts serious questions to retributivism. Like the previous group those who argue for this position do not expect the kingdom of God ever to be realized on earth, but on the other hand, they point out that we are commanded to pray for it, and that prayer has real effects. There are anticipations of the kingdom, forms of society which more nearly correspond to it than others. It is simply not the case that all forms of society are equidistant from God's will. In particular, a punitive society seems a poor reflection of the will of a God who seeks reconciliation. The apparatus of crime and punishment cannot be taken for granted and there is a question whether structures of mediation might not be a more appropriate way of dealing with offending. There is no single great theologian who is identified with this view but today it is identified above all with the Anabaptist, Mennonite or 'peace' churches. And, for those for whom proposing any theological connection with Rousseau will ring alarm bells, we can recall that the same Karl Barth who warned against the sluice gates of chaos also noted, at the end of his essay on Christian political responsibility, 'We bear no grudge against anyone who may have been reminded of Rousseau . . . We need not be ashamed of the affinity.' A progressive politics, especially with regard to criminal justice, is possible without any covert Pelagianism.

We will encounter these two perspectives throughout this book. They correspond with two readings of the Scriptures of Israel. The dominant post-Constantinian view (familiar to Anglican readers from the Book of Common Prayer) read these Scriptures from the

perspective of the king. God institutes kingship as God also institutes sacrifice and sacraments. All authority comes from God and is
exercised under God, to keep the order necessary for society to
survive. That this society is hierarchical and includes not just haves
and have-nots but, often enough, serfs or slaves, is part of the divine
order which is itself hierarchical. The Thirty-Nine Articles made this
plain in dispute with the Anabaptists. Kings have

> that only prerogative, which we see to have been given always
> to all godly Princes in holy Scripture by God himself; that is,
> that they should rule all estates and degrees committed to their
> charge by God . . . and restrain with the civil sword the
> stubborn and evildoers.

This need, the writers saw, was bound up with property, for the very
next article goes on:

> The Riches and Goods of Christians are not common, as
> touching the right, title and possession of the same, as certain
> Anabaptists do falsely boast. Notwithstanding, every man
> ought, of such things as he possesseth, liberally to give alms to
> the poor, according to his ability. (Articles XXXVII and XXXVIII,
> BCP)

In a hierarchical society justice is largesse.

The alternative view notes the profound critique of monarchy
within Scripture, especially on the part of the prophets. It notes
Deuteronomy's preference for a monarchy on the Scandinavian
model (Dt 17.15), where the monarch does his own shopping and is
not the peak of a hierarchical pyramid. More radically it asks, as
John Ball did, 'When Adam delved and Eve span, who was then the
gentleman?' In other words, it questions the assumption that class
division is inevitable and simply part of the created order. On the
hierarchical, or Hobbesian, view order is maintained by the sovereign. On the contrary view order is bound up with the recognition
of the right of every family to 'sit under its vine and fig tree', or in
other words, to have its equal share of the common wealth. Order
springs from equality and without equality there will only ever be
an armed truce between people and nations. For both views the
society God wants is a society at peace (Jer 29.11, where the NRSV

translates 'shalom' as 'welfare'). Peace, 'shalom' in Hebrew, is, I shall argue, the single most important theological category for understanding criminal justice. We need to look at it, therefore, in some detail.

Shalom

Old Testament scholars discern three strands in the use of shalom in the Hebrew Bible. In the first place it is, as it still is today in Semitic cultures, the normal word for greeting and parting. To reject this greeting is a serious matter (1 Sam 25.6f), a view Jesus himself reiterates (Mt 10.13–15; Lk 10.5–6, 10–12). The greeting 'peace' carries with it the promise of hospitality, of security and therefore trust. It also means well-being. Thus, Joseph in Egypt asks about the 'shalom' of his father, and Moses and his father-in-law enquire of each other's shalom (Gen 43.27; Ex 18.7). I shall use the Hebrew word 'shalom' in this book, rather than 'peace', because in English our word is largely negative – the absence of conflict – whereas in Hebrew the word has positive connotations of community well-being, of right relationships. Over and over again Scripture describes the loss of shalom and its re-establishment. We shall consider one such story, that of Joseph, in chapter eight. When peace is broken it is re-established by 'judging' (*shafat*), doing right, which is what Joseph does in checking that his brothers really have amended their behaviour.

A second strand of shalom in the Hebrew Bible is its extension beyond the immediate community to the nations and indeed to the whole cosmos. It is a special responsibility of the king, or as we might say later, the state (Ps 72). In this development the prophets of Israel repeatedly link peace and justice, to the extent that we can say that the connection is analytic. Thus Jeremiah says of Jerusalem:

This is the city that must be punished; there is nothing but oppression within her . . . violence and destruction are heard within her . . . For from the least to the greatest of them . . . everyone deals falsely. They have treated the wound of my people carelessly, saying 'Peace, peace', when there is no peace. (Jer 6.6, 7, 13–14)

Jeremiah is insisting that oppression of the poor, and the class divide which follows, is inconsistent with God's will, with shalom.

Isaiah promises:

> For the palace will be forsaken,
> The populous city deserted . . .
> Until a spirit from on high is poured out on us,
> And the wilderness becomes a fruitful field.
> Then [justice (*mishpat*)] will dwell in the wilderness,
> And righteousness abide in the fruitful field.
> The effect of [justice (*tsedequah*)] will be peace,
> and the result of justice, quietness and trust for ever.
>
> (Is 32.14–17)

The psalmist says:

> Let me hear what God the LORD will speak,
> For he will speak peace to his people, to his faithful . . .
> Steadfast love and faithfulness will meet;
> [Justice] and peace will kiss each other.
>
> (Ps 85.8, 10)

As with the personal greetings, 'shalom' is often, correctly, translated 'welfare' as when Jeremiah tells the exiles they must seek the shalom of Babylon, or that God's plans for Israel are for shalom, rather than for evil (Jer 29.7, 11).

Such peace is also bound up with what today we call criminal justice:

> These are the things that you shall do: Speak the truth to one another, render in your gates judgements [*mishpatim*] that are true and make for peace, do not devise evil in your hearts against one another, and love no false oath. (Zech 8.16–17)

A third strand in the use of shalom, arising from repeated disappointment, is its projection into the future:

> For to us a child is born,
> To us a son is given;
> And the government shall be upon his shoulder,

And his name shall be called
'Wonderful Counsellor, Mighty God,
Everlasting Father, Prince of Peace.'
(Is 9.6 RSV)

In a way which is crucial for our understanding of criminal justice, shalom is re-established after judgement but by forgiveness. Israel's sins are forgiven (Is 40.2) and God then re-establishes the covenant of peace (Is 54.10).

These promises were applied by the New Testament community to Jesus (Lk 1.79; 2.14). The need to use 'shalom' instead of 'peace' is emphasized by the fact that the peace Jesus brings is contrasted with the peace of the Pax Romana, a peace maintained by terror, so that the Roman historian Tacitus ironically remarks that the British tribes 'feared our peace'. This is the way in which the saying in Matthew 10.34–35 and John 14.27 is to be understood. Jesus does not endorse a false peace, based on domination, but biblical shalom, based on justice. It seems probable that Jesus' preferred phrase for God's project, 'the kingdom of God', embraces what was meant by 'shalom'. This is why Jesus says that the non-violent will inherit the earth (Mt 5.5) and why he insists on not resisting enemies and loving the enemy. Jesus concludes many of his encounters with the words, 'Go in peace'. His healing ministry both fulfils the messianic promises and, as a result, establishes shalom between people and between humankind and God. Jesus continues the tradition of linking peace and justice, as we see from the Beatitudes (Mt 5.9–11), a link we miss because the Greek word *dikaiosune* is usually trans-lated 'righteousness'. When we read, 'Blessed are those who hunger and thirst after justice,' or, 'Blessed are those who are persecuted for the sake of justice,' we realize that liberation theology has more evangelical warrant than has often been realized.

Paul, too, links the kingdom with the arrival of peace: 'The kingdom of God is not food and drink but righteousness and peace and joy in the Holy Spirit' (Rom 14.17). For this reason the pursuit of peace is mandated on Christians (Rom 14.19). The result of being justified is that 'we have peace with God through our Lord Jesus Christ' (Rom 5.1). Peace with God means reconciliation: 'For if while we were enemies, we were reconciled to God by the death of his Son, much more surely, having been reconciled, will we be saved by his life' (Rom 5.10). Here, too, we find a contrast between the peace of subjugation, the peace of Rome, and true peace, which springs from reconciliation. For the author of Ephesians, Christ has fulfilled the prophecy of Isaiah 57.19, and the cross has finally achieved peace between Jews and Gentiles:

> But now in Christ Jesus you who once were far off have been brought near by the blood of Christ. For he is our peace; in his flesh he has made both groups into one and has broken down the dividing wall, that is, the hostility between us. He has abolished the law with its commandments and ordinances, so that he might create in himself one new humanity in place of the two, thus making peace. (Eph 2.13–15)

The author is not speaking about some future state, the new creation, but about concrete social realities here and now. Shalom in this sense is a partial realization of the kingdom. It is something we can pray for and therefore work for. The early Christian communities understood themselves as a new people of peace. Citing Micah's prophecy that swords will be beaten into ploughshares Justin Martyr (*c.*150) commented, 'That has now come about.' This had implications for dealing with offenders as well for, following Paul's example in the Corinthian correspondence, these communities dealt with offences within their ranks by what is now called 'reintegrative shaming'. The promise of peace, and the sense that it is something realized here and now, which has real social consequences, has implications for criminal justice because all punishment involves violence. The key question for any Christian reflection on criminal justice is what the command to love our enemies means for the criminal justice process. The love of enemies is designed as a way of breaking the spiral of violence, of responding to harm without doing harm in return. It is, as Moltmann has said, a true ethic of responsibility, a way of extending our responsibility to our enemies (Moltmann, 1990, p. 131). After Constantine it became increasingly difficult for Christians to see how to do that both in relation to conflict between kingdoms, but also in criminal justice. That the Sermon on the Mount might have had implications for the latter seems scarcely to have been guessed until the Anabaptists insisted on it.

Shalom, social order and criminal justice

In his famous account of the rise of the prison, Michel Foucault begins with the story of the execution by torture of the regicide Damiens in 1757, but let us begin a little further back in the world of the Book of Common Prayer. This world had large and notorious prisons, like the Marshalsea and Newgate, but they were not prisons in the modern sense. Apart from the debtors' prison, most prisons were lock-ups, where people were kept pending trial. Social order was maintained by the monarch in council, and later by Parliament. Hobbes' *Leviathan* appeared at just the moment (1651) when what would later be called the absolute or omnicompetent state was beginning to appear.

With the exception of the Anabaptists, who judged it inconsistent with the gospel either to serve as magistrates or to go to court, the need for punishment seems to have been taken for granted by most of society (though the protests in Shakespeare's *King Lear* are interesting). During the eighteenth and the early nineteenth centuries some of the cruellest punishments, such as mutilation and burning, were abandoned, as too were shame punishments, and imprisonment became the norm. The understanding of imprisonment has swung between two poles since then. The Baptist John Howard, who became famous throughout Europe for his reports on prisons, and the rationalist Beccaria, equally believed prisons should be useful places in which people were reformed by education, constructive work and the opportunity for reflection. By the second decade of the next century the treadmill was in use, and by the third the emphasis had shifted to providing hard bed and hard board. A punitive philosophy was in place throughout the middle of the nineteenth century. The end of that century, however, saw the emergence of what came to be called 'penal welfarism', the view that crime must be understood in its social context, that criminals must be reformed and reintegrated into the community, that social changes and particularly greater egalitarianism can do much to eliminate crime. A whole host of factors underlay this view: a realization of the suffering industrial capitalism had brought to the poor, the trades union movement and the struggle for universal suffrage, later the impact of the First World War and then the effects of the Depression. These two events in particular meant that society was viewed as a whole, and not hierarchically. If all, willy nilly, could die for 'freedom' and if millions could be rendered unemployed not because they were feckless but because of the malfunctionings of 'the market' then this suggested that all were bound together in weal and woe and all were profoundly responsible one for another. Such understandings found political expression in the Welfare State in Britain and other European countries and in the New Deal in the United States. Penal welfarism was the crime policy which accompanied these developments, given classic expression by none other than Winston Churchill as early as 1911 in his famous remark that a society is to be judged by the way in which it deals with offenders. With some difference of emphasis penal welfarism was shared by governments of both the left and the right, socialist and conservative, Republican and Democrat. It represented, in some respects, a commitment to what I have called 'shalom', an account of peace and the common good. Solutions to crime were to be found within the community. By the 1960s the call was for decentralization, a distrust of both experts and institutions. This broad consensus began to break down in the 1970s and has been systematically undone since then. There were many reasons for this collapse. In the first place the optimism and belief in progress which marked the Enlightenment, and which found expression in penal welfare, was deeply damaged by the Holocaust. Utopia was replaced by dystopia, from Orwell to Huxley to Attwood. Second, the unparalleled rise in living standards in the West in the three decades following the Second World War was not matched by the promised fall in crime. On the contrary, crime rates rose exponentially. The penal welfarist link between crime and social conditions was therefore argued to be false. Those who argued for alternatives to prison and hard treatment seemed to have nothing new to offer. At the same time some liberals questioned the goal of 'treatment', suspecting sinister designs of normalization and thought control, and complaining that the integrity and autonomy of prisoners was not being respected. Liberal, well-intentioned reforms, it was argued, simply led to more repression and coercion. The call had been for destructuring but in fact state control became stronger. The rhetoric spoke of therapy but the reality was one of power. These discontents presaged a change in cultural mood in the course of which there was a return to retributivism, and it once more became respectable to be punitive. Out went treatment and in came deterrence, incapacitation, the need for law and order. In Britain in the decade between

1993 and 2003 a series of Home Secretaries have outbid each other in their zeal to be 'tough on crime'. Michel Foucault spoke of the 'great incarceration' in the nineteenth century but he, had he lived, would have been astonished to see a new and far greater incarceration at the end of the twentieth century. In the United States criminologists are speaking of a new gulag archipelago, with 2 million people imprisoned at any given time and another 3.5 million on probation or parole. In Britain and the rest of Europe prison numbers are likewise at record highs and prison-building programmes are constantly expanding.

Sociologists of crime like Stanley Cohen (1985), Jock Young (1999) and David Garland (2001) help us to understand these phenomena. They are, of course, bound up with the economic changes which have taken place over the past thirty years which we know, collectively, as 'globalization'. This stands for the transition from industrial to finance capital, made possible by information technology, the control of almost three-quarters of world trade by corporations, the end of the 'job for life', and the rise of the 'risk society' in which, among other things, the middle classes find themselves more vulnerable to crime. This world has seen the gap between rich and poor rise throughout the world, a fact which has been enhanced by tax policies which privilege the rich while targeting 'welfare scroungers'. As Garland puts it, what has emerged is a deeply divided society, 'with one sector being deregulated in the name of market enterprise and another disciplined in the name of market morality' (Garland, 2001, p. 101). In this situation it has been the case both that street crime and disorder have increased and that crime has assumed a new political significance. Egged on by the mass media, for which crime is always a selling point, and for which crime dramas provide a staple form of entertainment, politicians are able to deflect questions about social justice by blaming problems on 'crime'. The penal welfare consensus has been replaced by a twofold strategy. On the one hand there is an instrumental criminology driven by economics, which wants results which are cheapest for the taxpayer. This assumes that criminal behaviour is to be expected because humans are by nature, not inclined to hate both God and their neighbour, but 'rational utility maximizers' – in other words, always going to take the chance to make a fast buck if they can. On the other hand there is a criminology which demonizes the criminal – we only have to think about the hysteria around paedophilia in Britain at the moment – and casts criminals as uniquely vicious and irreformable. What has been lost between these two, as Garland points out, is the excluded middle of the disadvantaged or poorly socialized offender whom it is the task of the whole of society to reintegrate. This rests in turn on a change in the understanding of human nature from an optimistic 'Enlightenment' belief that people are amenable to being resocialized or re-educated to a belief that people are not very easily changed after all. In place of penal welfare came penal realism which celebrated sobriety and wanted to forget utopia. Augustine was right after all. On the other hand we might argue that what has been lost is a vision of shalom. Exactly as the prophets argued, shalom, peace and justice for the whole of society, is unattainable if levels of division go beyond certain levels. The social policy which has followed the economic changes of the late twentieth century, however, is Social Darwinism writ large, a winner-takes-all world in which, as we know, the richest three billionaires earn more than the poorest 600 million fellow human beings, or the richest Mexican more than the poorest 17 million of his fellow citizens. In such a situation, as Margaret Thatcher accurately remarked, there is no such thing as society, and there cannot be shalom either. As Young (1999) has argued, we have moved from a society which sought to be inclusive, and to reintegrate offenders, to a bulimic society which spews them out and which is in principle exclusive. The rhetoric is one of war, on drugs or on crime, and the police are 'the front line'. Those on the receiving end are the poor who are regarded with 'fear and loathing'. The middle class, it has been argued, those whose votes are most courted by politicians, are particularly prone to punish as the underclass constitute their feckless 'other' and seem to act out all the things which, but for the disciplines of social restraint, they might want to act out themselves. They are, therefore, predisposed to exclusionary processes. This same middle class, of course, largely accounts for church membership. That the poor are increasingly warehoused in prisons only makes more evident what was already true, that they do not belong to the community. Despite the rhetoric of being 'tough on the causes of crime' the strategy for dealing with offenders is better detection, higher rates of imprisonment and greater penal severity. Although it ought to be obvious, the abstractness of much discussion of crime and punishment obscures the fact that the nature of community and the nature of the economy determine, to a large extent, the shape of penal policy. These facts, and this situation, form the indispensable background to our reflections, in the following chapters, on law and criminal justice.

The chapters which follow all relate to key words in the Christian Scriptures: law, justice, sin, punishment, scapegoat, victim, forgiveness, church. That was not my original plan but as the book began to take shape I found this to be the case and it simply confirms the huge place ideas of crime and punishment have in our founding documents. Dealing with each (interrelated) issue I have tried to relate the theological discussion to ongoing discussions within the field of criminal justice and penal reform. The nature of the series is not to include the detailed footnoting of an academic text, but I have included a note of the sources I have found most helpful, the sources for my own discussion, in the suggestions for further reading.

2 | Law and the Life of the Community

In what is one of the central images of the Jewish and Christian Scriptures, God gives the law and commandments to Moses, written on tablets of stone (Ex 24.12). According to the psalmist the law of the Lord is perfect, and revives the soul (Ps 19.7), while those who love the law have shalom (Ps 119.165). 'Law' is a scriptural key word, occurring more than two hundred times in the Hebrew Bible, where it mostly translates *Torah*, though also *mishpat*, judgement. What is meant by 'law' in these instances is a mixture of what has come to be distinguished as criminal, civil and cultic law. Some of it is so-called 'apodeictic' law, God's absolute command, which simply has to be obeyed, while some of it is case law. All of it is set in the narrative frame of the Exodus and the settlement of Israel in Canaan. The narrative frame is essential: it establishes that the purpose of the law is to continue to guarantee freedom from slavery. Failure to obey the law leads to slavery in either the literal or the moral sense. In the New Testament, law is found thirty times in the Gospels (where of course many uses are doublets), but more than one hundred times in Paul, and above all in Romans. Partly through Paul's complex polemics 'law' has an ambivalent resonance in Western society, but for Israel, law is the heart of God's self-giving to history. It is God's self-expression and it is life-giving. It is entirely consistent with this that Jesus insists that he has not come to abolish the law but to fulfil it (Mt 5.17). In his debate with his fellow Jews about whether or not Gentiles formed part of the new body, which he called 'ecclesia', Paul was led to a dense dialectic in reflecting on where law stood in God's purposes. On the one hand, as 'a Pharisee of the Pharisees' Paul believed that the law was 'holy and just and good' (Rom 7.12). He had no desire whatever to proclaim it a dead letter. On the other hand he could write that, 'The law works wrath' (Rom 4.15), or, 'By the works of the law no one is justified' (Gal 2.16), because in his view law alone did not effect salvation, could not produce the shalom he looked for (Gal 4.23).

Since Luther's time Romans has become the heart of Protestantism's canon, and this has probably intensified the consciousness of law within the Church. Many Anglican churches continue the Prayer Book practice of beginning the eucharist with a summary of 'the law', concluding: 'Lord, write all these laws in our hearts, we beseech you.' What is the connection between this scriptural talk of law and the law about which Home Secretaries or Attorney Generals speak, the police enforce, and solicitors, barristers and judges interpret and apply? I shall begin by looking at one of the Greek words sometimes translated 'law', namely *ethos*, custom.

Law and custom

'Ethos', custom or way of life, has passed into English as a description of the felt values of a given culture. These customs or values are normative, which is why Jesus, and later Stephen, are accused of endangering the ethos of the Jewish people (Mk 2.23ff; Acts 6.14). At the same time Jesus respects these traditions (Lk 4.16). Humans are community creatures, and their fragility, their complex needs for food, clothing and shelter, defence, friendship, ritual and creativity, all mean that structure is as vital to them as oxygen. Where anarchy has reigned for long periods it seems always to have been a disaster for the weak. As a somewhat suspect witness, John Locke put it: 'That ill deserves the name of confinement which hedges us in only from bogs and precipices . . . For in all the states of created beings capable of laws, where there is no law, there is no freedom.' The psalmist's sense that only those who love the law have peace is only too well exemplified in contemporary Russia, in Angola or indeed, as I write, in the Shankill Road. The Brazilian film *City of God*, based on a true story, presents a dystopian vision of gang warfare in a Rio barrio at the beginning of the third millennium. It depicts a society where guns are readily available, where children become addicted to violence and killing, and where, in Lear's words, 'man's life's as cheap as beast's'. In such situations there is indeed no such thing as society and, as Locke argued, where there is no law there is no freedom. This explains the apparent paradox that those politicians who lay the greatest weight on the freedom of the individual to do what they please have at the same time the greatest commitment to 'law and order' and spend most on policing.

That we can recognize such situations as dystopian makes the point that fortunately they are not the norm. Lewis Mumford spoke of the origin of ethics as lying in the life-conserving practices of the village. What we find in Proverbs 12 and following are expressions of such a life-conserving ethos. In any society proverbs distil common-sense wisdom and unwritten codes. Born into a society you grow up with such unwritten codes as a sixth sense. The punishment for breaking these codes is usually ostracism, rejection or shame. Even exceptionally permissive societies like those of Western Europe at the beginning of the third millennium have such codes though they may vary from class to class and sub-group to sub-group. In every society they perform the vital function of regulating the conduct of everyday life, and above all the relation of the sexes. In a society where most things are allowed there remains, for example, profound social disapproval both of male violence against women and any behaviour which takes advantage of children. This is not to say, of course, that these things do not happen, but it is to say that no man could go into a pub and boast that he was doing them. To do so would be to court certain ostracism and possible violence. Of course we need to distinguish between silent pressure to conform and the exercise of power by an elite. Societies are usually governed by a combination of force and authority, of coercive habit and legitimate consent.

The power of a cultural ethos is immense, and it is no surprise that some jurists consider law to originate in the codified custom of a society. 'When a thing is done again and again', says Thomas Aquinas, 'it seems to proceed from a deliberate judgement of reason. Accordingly custom has the force of law, abolishes law and is the interpreter of law' (*ST* 1a.2ae 97.3). Aquinas is certainly right for English law where some ancient laws have been established not by enactment but by custom. Of course it is also true, as Aquinas goes on to recognize, that customs are never static. Customs change as modes of production change, and in relation to patterns of employment, belief and education. Customs are tenacious and long-lasting, but the sense of inter-generational tension which was already a cliché in the sixteenth century, as Shakespeare makes clear in his Comedies, shows how they are always under pressure and changing subtly. The customs of the older generation seem passé to the next and are modified as this generation comes to maturity.

It is also true, of course, that an ethos is not necessarily life-conserving, and may sometimes be downright dehumanizing –

think of the ethos of Hitler's Germany or Pinochet's Chile or Botha's South Africa, for example. Perhaps few societies are as bad as these. In most there are rules or traditions for nurturing the sick, the old, the weak and the stranger. At the same time part of the job of the Christian doctrine of original sin is to insist that there are no societies where the ethos perfectly corresponds with God's will. This is the reason that Jesus and his followers got across the ethos of their contemporaries, challenged their structure of feeling. With the possible exception of a few hunter-gatherer groups every society is deeply distorted by gender, class and ethnic biases. When Paul spoke of a society in which there was 'no Jew or Greek, male or female, bond or free' (Gal 3.28) he was thinking of the movement which sprang from Jesus as the seedbed of a new humanity, structured around a quite new ethos. Paul was gripped by a strong sense of the dawn of a new age, in which the promise of Jeremiah's covenant, where the law is written on every person's heart, was realized, and he seems to have expected his communities to live accordingly. In his dispute with the Pharisees Jesus had contrasted conformist behaviour with the way in which the heart feels, and Paul seems to have built on this distinction. One of his suspicions of law corresponds to later legal reflection about internal and external behaviour. A man may be deterred from rape by the thought of a long prison sentence, but he may nevertheless fantasize about it. His behaviour is not illegal but it is immoral. The man who finds the very idea of rape abhorrent in view of his respect for women as people is the truly moral individual. Paul's sense of the new covenant and the new creation seeks to go beyond law and has thus fed a utopian and anarchist strand in the history of the Church which has never quite been silenced and which always constitutes a challenge to those who celebrate the gift of law. Before the end of the first century the Pastoral Epistles already represent a compromise between this new ethos and the prevailing ethos of society, deeply structured by race, class and patriarchy.

If we ask about the relation of custom to criminal law today, and what kind of theological significance this has the answer must be, as mentioned in the previous chapter, in terms of structures of affect. As we have just seen, custom may often be dehumanizing, but customs change and one of the pressures for change is the life and teaching of the Church. In much of the world, perhaps arguably throughout the world, ethos, moral common sense, owes much to the New Testament. At this foundational level, therefore, the gospel bears on the law.

The emergence of law

Small, simple societies, such as hunter-gatherer societies, survive without law. In them the sanctions of custom are sufficient. Law, the recognition of sanctions which are universally binding in a given society, emerges as society becomes more complex. In his *Second Treatise on Government*, Locke imagines the emergence of law in this way: in the state of nature, he argues:

> There wants an establish'd, settled, known Law, received and allowed by common consent to be the Standard of Right and Wrong, and the common measure to decide all controversies between them . . . Secondly, In the State of Nature there wants a Known and indifferent Judge, with Authority to determine all differences according to the established law . . . Thirdly, in the state of Nature there often wants Power to back and support the Sentence when right, and to give it due Execution.

The 'state of nature' is his account of what I have called small, simple societies. The emergence of law is, then, part of that critical move which includes the emergence of cities, an increase in the division of labour, the evolution of social hierarchy, and perhaps of patriarchy, which some feminists have read as the world-historical 'fall'. Law, as opposed to custom, is the public enactment of codes which have to be obeyed. As we have seen, all societies, no matter how simple, are constituted by drawing boundaries which ought not to be transgressed, by defining behaviour which is, or is not, acceptable. There are no societies where anything goes. Tellingly, the Greek word *nomos* has its roots in the verb to distribute, and is used to speak of the allocation of pasture among different members of the community. In origin it is literally about boundaries. With the emergence of law, as opposed to custom, such boundaries are, to use the Hebrew mythology, carved in stone as a symbol that they are universally available for consultation, so that no member of the society can say that they are not aware of their prescriptions.

On this account it might be argued that law is a necessary function of a complex society. For all his anarchic leanings Paul's sense that 'the law is holy, just and good' (Rom 7.12) is often right, because every complex society has found the need to enact laws to prevent the terrible tensions introduced by human selfishness, folly and violence tearing it apart. Laws, on this understanding, set out the minimum conditions for life together and in this sense law can be life-giving. The 'can be' there is deliberately cautious. We have noted already the way cultural ethos changes, and laws with it. One of the major lessons of the twentieth century was that such changes are not necessarily in a more humane direction. Cultures can suffer catastrophic moral collapse and use law to enforce barbarism. Paul's ambivalence about the law was more than justified, and the argument that law is life-giving can never be taken for granted.

The concern for what it is which enables and sustains human community is one of the areas in which law and religion come together. Both law and religion embody normative views of the human, moral perceptions which underwrite a vision of human community. Whether in simple or complex industrial or post-industrial societies the task of law is to protect people against violence, cruelty and the misappropriation of their property. Ideally, and in line with its function in Hebrew Scripture, law is especially concerned with protecting the vulnerable and has also, until recently, sought to protect religious customs and institutions. The blasphemy laws, which came into prominence over the Rushdie fatwa, are an instance of this. Since prevention is better than cure law seeks to prevent undesirable behaviour, whether behaviour which is physically damaging or likely to be shocking to the community, dangerous or simply inconvenient (like some parking restrictions). Law also functions to further the maintenance of society's common life by enforcing revenue collection, seeing that every child receives schooling, or that every employee receives a minimum wage, and so on.

The medieval historian R. W. Southern remarks that in the Middle Ages people sought liberty by increasing the number of rules under which they lived. That seems strange to those of us who are more familiar with the 'iron cage' of bureaucracy, constantly complaining (in Europe) about EU regulations or in the United States about federal bureaucracy, but if we imagine a system where the will of the local lord is absolute we can see why Locke could believe that law can free us and promise a less arbitrary life. Law can support the weak, enabling them to gain rights which the power structure of society would make impossible. Labour legislation over the past century and a half is a good example of this and complaints by employers' organizations like the Confederation of British Industry about policies such as the minimum wage show that this is still a very live issue. When functioning properly law is, then, salvific. It 'redeems' from chaos and provides protection for the weak against the strong. In recognition of this most societies seem to have ascribed the law ultimately to God, and certainly Israel did so. The nineteenth-century sociologist Durkheim thought of this as a case of projection: society absolutized its will and called this 'God'. Durkheim argued that all cultures have a 'collective consciousness' which is made up of the totality of beliefs and sentiments common to the average members of a society, and that this consciousness changes slowly and links successive generations to one another. Law originates in what he calls 'mechanical solidarity', the solidarity of simple societies where everyone knows everyone. In such societies, he argued, law is penal, repressive and religious. In industrial society, by contrast, we have 'organic solidarity' based on freely chosen co-operation between individuals and here law has purely restitutory sanctions. Law is the codification of a culture's collective consciousness and an act is criminal when it offends it. The identification of the offended party in criminal prosecutions as 'the Crown', in Britain, or as 'the people' in the United States, might be understood as an expression of this view. Crime is an offence against the collective will. This will has a virtually religious aspect: it has the authority vested in earlier societies in kings and priests, which accounts for the quasi-religious paraphernalia which surrounds the operation of law. Later I shall put critical questions to this account but I note here its prima facie plausibility.

Law as command

In what Durkheim called 'advanced societies' the idea of law is taken for granted, and we rarely question its meaning. For philosophers of law, on the other hand, it remains a puzzle, and is still a subject of keen debate. What exactly is law? One suggestion is that law is an order backed by threats, the order deriving ultimately from 'the sovereign' (e.g. Parliament or Congress). Broadly speaking this way of understanding law is known as 'legal positivism'. In ancient Israel, and still today in some Muslim countries, the sovereign, the one who ultimately promulgates law, is assumed to be God. The problem with all such theocracies, as the debates in the Hebrew Bible make clear, concerns the interpretation of the command. Deuteronomy, which is a root and branch revision of Israelite law, casts itself in the fiction of 'the authentic account' of what happened to Moses on Sinai. It needed to do this, presumably, to gain credence with those who remembered the law differently and who disagreed.

Since the mid-seventeenth century, contract theory has suggested that citizens make a deal with the executive whereby they agree that the executive should pass laws in return for peace and security. Beccaria's account of law, cited in the first chapter, is a good example. In a representative democracy 'the people' is technically sovereign, and so passes its own laws which every voting member supposedly agrees to abide by. This democratic account should not blind us to the extent to which law continues to have 'divine' attributes, such as being autonomous, self-sustaining and independent of any exterior reality (Fitzpatrick, 1992). 'Law', as referred to by judges and magistrates, is commonly set above psychological, sociological or medical knowledge as when judges in rape trials pronounce on what normal male and female behaviour is, or when magistrates denigrate the relevance of social work reports. From this standpoint it is 'the law' which is supposed to right the wrongs in society. The need for specialists, the arcane aspect of the law which cannot be grasped by lay people is, it is argued, redolent of religion. One could object that, in a democracy, law is constantly made and amended but there is certainly something in the charge that law remains 'hedged with divinity' and the aesthetics of the courtroom are designed to emphasize this.

The judiciary are not elected but, in the British context, are servants of the Crown, which means public servants. Parliament makes law but judges interpret it. In doing so they may find it necessary to criticize the law-making body. In Britain, recently, for example, the action of Home Secretaries in detaining some murderers beyond their prescribed tariff has been condemned by the courts as unlawful. This critical function of law is one of the most important checks and balances in a democracy. Whenever governments veer towards tyranny the legal profession can become a dangerous place, as, for example, in Zimbabwe today, where human rights lawyers have been savagely tortured.

The idea of law as command is also illuminated by Durkheim's suggestion that law codifies the collective consciousness of a culture. It helps explain the idea of 'the majesty of the law', or what biblical scholars call 'apodeictic law' – law which comes with an absolute command, the breach of which incurs the severest penalties, and often death. If you trespass on what is considered to be sacred, you can expect a severe response. The Ten Commandments are understood as law in this sense. The idea of law as command is less illuminating as a way to understand case law, which comprises the bulk of the law codes in the Old Testament and forms the basis of the English legal system. This is a much more pragmatic affair, constantly testing itself against the collective consciousness, constantly being renegotiated, never finalized. More problematic still is the extent to which we may in fact speak of a collective consciousness, and this is perhaps the most far-reaching objection to Durkheim's account. Even if we think of the murder of the two-year-old James Bulger by two ten- and eleven-year-olds, a case which certainly mobilized a very profound sense of moral outrage in Britain, it cannot be said there was any agreement as to what ought to be done with the offenders. Diametrically opposite views were urged, and the insistence of the courts on the attempt to rehabilitate the killers almost certainly did not represent a majority view.

Law as a collection of rules

In a democracy it feels odd to speak of law as the command of a sovereign. Rather, it has been suggested, we should think of law as a system of rules we democratically agree to be normed by. Humans, it is argued, are rule-making and rule-following creatures. There are no games without rules, and the commonest operations of life, from courting to trade, all depend on rules. We grow up learning rules of behaviour and what we call law is simply an extension of this rule-governed behaviour. If the law is to treat its citizens as rational and responsible agents, it is argued, it must be an enterprise of subjecting human conduct to the governance of rules. There are informal rules (for eating, for example, which vary widely from country to country); there are prohibitions, like the Table of Kindred and Affinity at the end of the Book of Common Prayer, which entertained countless generations when the sermon was boring by leading people to muse on who they were forbidden to marry; and there are substantive rules which lay down (usually) what must not be done. On one account there are primary rules, which are the expression of the moral sense of a culture, and then these are articulated by secondary rules, which form the substance of the criminal law. The second kind of rules set penalties and outline procedures. Those making the law have to ask whether it should be used to penalize this or that sort of behaviour – changes in the obscenity laws or abortion laws are examples of areas which were once criminal and are so no longer. In this process there is a dialectic between primary and secondary rules, as the law-making process affects a culture's ethos, and as the laws, or secondary rules, are changed to reflect those changes in turn.

Whether this suggestion for understanding law gets away from the imperiousness of command is a moot point. As noted earlier, law assumes its own autonomy and operates from a position of domination. Behind the picture of the rule-following reflective subject is another narrative of the dominance of official determinations which are tacitly assumed to be a universal necessity by appeal to the Hobbesian primal scene. Rather than being explained by our propensity to follow a rule, law is actually accounted for by this myth, which is manipulative. The individual supposedly consents to be normed by rules but is in fact coerced into accepting laws which express domination. Feminists, for example, complain that the law's definition of rape takes precedence over women's experience of it. In its appeal to a supposed universal necessity the account of law as rule-following is actually a form of positivism (Fitzpatrick, 1992).

Whether we accept this critique will depend on how sanguine we are about the processes of participatory democracy. Social contract theory, to be sure, emerged when such democracy was very rudimentary indeed and the law was rather nakedly an instrument of social control. The nineteenth- and twentieth-century struggles for universal suffrage and labour rights should not be underestimated, and there is no doubt that law is now more democratic than it was. On the other hand, in the West at any rate, it continues to be both made and administered largely by those in social classes one and two and so the charge of domination is not self-evidently absurd.

Law and the vindication of rights

As opposed to both forms of positivism other legal philosophers, and especially Ronald Dworkin, argue that law should be understood as a matter of politico-moral principles. Principles are fundamental to legal argument in a way that rules are not, which is easily illustrated by looking at hard cases. Here judges decide not by appealing to rules, which they can do in non-controversial cases, but by appealing to principles endorsed by the community as a whole (Dworkin, 1978, 1986).

On this account the specific task of law is to champion individual rights against the Government. Rights are not a gift of God but spring from the idea of a shared human dignity on the one hand, the supposition that there are ways of treating someone which are inconsistent with recognizing them as a full member of the human community, and the assumption of political equality which supposes that the weaker members of a community are entitled to the same concern and respect as the more powerful, on the other. We recognize that law necessarily expresses the majority's view of the common good. The institution of rights, by contrast, represents the majority's promise to the minority that their dignity and equality will be respected. It is the task of judges to administer the law in the interests of individual rights. Judges are the princes of law's empire, the capitals of which are the courts, and legal philosophers are the seers and prophets. Law is in principle a utopian exercise which helps move society on to a better future. It is essentially a matter of a 'protestant attitude' which requires each citizen to be responsible for imagining what his or her society's commitments to principle are.

The emphasis on 'every citizen' belies the central thrust of the argument, which is that law is essentially the business of its practitioners, and especially judges. Law is, Dworkin argues, argumentative and interpretative – but it is argument and interpretation between 'experts'. They play a large part in constructing social reality. 'Law's empire', it turns out, is administered by a sort of secular priesthood, who have 'the last word' in their interpretation of law. The hallmark of law is integrity, which requires government to extend the same standards of justice to all. Where there is unfairness in law we can expect the interpretive approach to gradually iron it out.

That law is essentially a hermeneutic exercise is beyond doubt. What is more questionable is, first, the privileging of the role of the legal profession, class-based on one side of the Atlantic and commercially driven on the other, second the abstraction from the realities of power in society, and third the tacit assumption of the rightness of liberal individualism. Law is certainly a politico-moral enterprise, but it is open to understand this in a quite different, more communitarian or, to use an old-fashioned word, socialist, direction.

Law as education

As a man of his time Thomas Aquinas (*c.*1225–1274) argued that monarchy was the best form of government, but interestingly his account of law is not framed in terms of command. He brought together biblical and Aristotelian insights on law and wedded them to Roman ideas of jurisprudence. Roman law distinguished civil law, the ancient customary law of Rome, the 'law of the nations' which arose out of the need to adjudicate between Romans and non-Romans, and the natural law, supposedly acceptable and self-evident to members of any human community. He argued that there was a hierarchy of eternal, natural and human law. The eternal law is an expression of God's being, justice being one of the divine attributes. Natural law is the imprint of eternal law on created things and we learn from it how to behave. By virtue of this imprint we know 'by nature' that good is to be done and evil to be avoided. All other precepts of natural law are based on this. Human law, on the other hand, is the use of our reason to regulate our everyday affairs. Every genuine law is derived from natural law and the end of law is the common good. Law has an essential educative function:

> The purpose of human law is to lead men to virtue, not suddenly but gradually. Wherefore it does not lay upon the multitude of imperfect men the burdens of those who are already virtuous, that they should abstain from all evil. To those young people who are inclined to acts of virtue, by their good natural disposition, or by custom, or rather by the gift of God, paternal training suffices, which is by admonitions. But since some are found to be depraved, and prone to vice, and not easily amenable to words, it was necessary for such to be restrained from evil by force and fear, in order that, at least they might desist from evil-doing, and leave others in peace, and that they themselves, by being habituated in this way, might be brought to do willingly what hitherto they did from fear, and thus become virtuous. Now this kind of training,

which compels through fear of punishment, is the discipline of laws. (*ST* 1.a.2ae 95.1)

Aquinas' suggestion that the community is educated by law was followed by the Reformers, who discerned a threefold use of the law. The law convicts us of unrighteousness, curbs those who, unless forced, have no regard for rectitude and justice, and helps believers learn with greater truth and certainty what the will of the Lord is which they aspire to follow. The Reformers kept the idea of natural law, which included, in their view, obedience to all those in authority. They argued that we know by the natural light that we are made for civil society and that offences which harm civil society should be punished. On the other hand our understanding is darkened by sin and therefore natural law must be subordinated to biblical law. The best summary of this was the Ten Commandments, from which every prescript of civil and criminal law was ingeniously derived.

The idea that law has a pedagogic function again carries conviction. We can think, for example, of laws relating to drunk driving, or to racial or sexual harassment which have, arguably, served to conscientize society as a whole to adopt less dangerous behaviour or offensive attitudes. In a secular democracy the source of this pedagogy will be understood as some kind of very approximate summary of the collective consciousness.

Natural law

The idea that good laws are rooted in natural law remains a matter of keen debate among legal philosophers to this day. The idea was originally Stoic, arising from their belief that divine rationality expressed itself in every part of the cosmos. It came into the Christian bloodstream through Cicero, who was constantly cited by theologians right up to the Reformation. It was incorporated in Justinian's codification of law in the sixth century and then reworked in the thirteenth century by Aquinas who added Aristotelian ideas to the Stoic view, so that what was 'natural' was that which fulfilled its proper purpose. The idea of natural law offered a view of law as eternal and absolutely valid. A growing historical sense, aware of the culturally relative nature of justice, problematized this, and a growing scepticism about the divine, manifested by thinkers like Voltaire or Hume, replaced the idea of divine law with that of subjective or social truth. Legal positivism, in the nineteenth century, in understanding law as no more than the command of the sovereign, opened the way for complete relativism.

Though condemned as a piece of scholastic obscurantism natural law had to be rescued in Germany after the Second World War in order to deal with those who had committed monstrous crimes which were legal within the framework of the Third Reich. The idea of natural law provides a society with criteria by which to judge state law. Appeal to Scripture might perform the same function, and did in fact do so in relation to the pass laws in South Africa.

The problem with natural law is in specifying what constitutes it. The contemporary Thomist philosopher John Finnis, who argues for the centrality of natural law, identifies a set of basic goods (life, knowledge, play, friendship, aesthetic experience, practical reason-ableness and religion) and a list of basic principles of practical reasoning, such as formulating a rational plan of life, having no arbitrary preferences between persons and never choosing to act directly against a basic good, which he claims are self-evident. These goods and principles constitute the natural law and, exactly as Aquinas argued, positive law, to be moral, must derive from it 'like conclusions from general premises'. The legislator stands to the natural law as a builder does to an architect: he or she fills in the detail of the rules and regulations while remaining within the principles of the natural law.

Finnis' account of basic goods illustrates one of the central problems with the idea of natural law. Either the goods are so general that it is difficult to see how positive law can be properly derived from it or, as the Enlightenment philosophers argued, they are obviously culture specific. It can also be objected that, as in the Lutheran idea that it includes obedience to superiors, it often seems to articulate the ideas of the status quo. Moreover the nature of the human good is not universally agreed, as present-day disputes about whether or not to accept human rights conventions show. At the same time there are a set of 'truths held to be self-evident' which, as the positivist Hart argued, cluster around the facts of human vulner-ability, the assumption of human equality, the assumption that all people have limited abilities, a limited will to do the good and limited resources which do make sense of the idea of natural law and to which jurists still appeal. We may choose, with St Thomas, to root these assumptions in the Eternal Law, which is to say in God, but in fact they are fairly minimal assumptions which any secularist can sign up to. From the theological point of view this is precisely their problem because, it can be said, they define the common good too thinly, and therefore do not yield a set of laws which are distinctively Christian. On the other hand they do tell us, as Barth, no advocate of natural law, remarked, that even the pagan, civil community is still in the kingdom of Christ.

Law and morality

As we have seen, law changes as ethos changes. To take a familiar example, a century ago homosexuality incurred both intense social disapprobation and was a criminal offence. Sixty years after the jailing of Oscar Wilde Parliament decided that what passed between consenting adults was not a matter for the criminal law, though the Law Lords later took the view that this did not extend to sado-masochistic practices. Today, in most sections of society, though unfortunately not in the Church, it is prejudice against homosexuals which incurs disapprobation. Another example is the Gove Land Rights case in Australia in 1971 where the judge decided that eighteenth-century English law did not apply because its view of land ownership was 'false in fact and *unacceptable in our society*'. The judge here was effectively marking a change in moral perception. The same applies to the invocation of science to underwrite law. In the 1930s supposedly scientific eugenics, accepted by wide sections of the community, underwrote the Jim Crow laws. Today it is generally accepted that the 'science' which supported these laws was itself racist.

The connection between law and morality has sometimes been understood very strictly. The Lutheran Reformation believed that legal decisions were moral decisions, and that judges needed to consult Scripture and pray before making judgements. Assize sermons in Britain frequently reminded judges of the solemnity of their duty. Today the connection between law and morality is more a matter of debate. Legal positivism, which reached its acme in the early nineteenth century, believed that moral questions had nothing to do with law. Such a view is counter-intuitive but it arises not just from legal absolutism but from its opposite, the need to take account of unjust laws, a need I shall return to in a moment. Also, there are many forms of immoral behaviour about which we do not legislate, on the grounds that such behaviour does not damage society sufficiently to come within the scope of legal enactment. To use Herbert Hart's example, the difference between law and morality can be illustrated by comparing the difference between saying that such and such will be illegal as from the first of January and saying that such and such will be immoral. The first happens all the time, but the second would be impossible (Hart, 1961). Despite these difficulties the connection between law and morality cannot ultimately be surrendered, especially in a pluralistic society where the question of what is right and wrong may ultimately be decided by law. As R. A. Duff has argued, legal obligation is a species of moral obligation (Duff, 1986). Law makes a moral claim on our obedience. The obligations which the laws of my community impose on me are aspects of my moral obligation to care for the good of that community – a view which takes us back to Aquinas, for whom the common good lies at the heart of law.

Unjust law

In speaking of law as command, of its expression of the collective consciousness and of its educative function all the time I have been skirting a colossal difficulty which lies at the heart of the New Testament narrative and therefore of Paul's ambivalence. As I mentioned just now, this is the existence of unjust law.

In Galatians Paul is engaged in a complex argument with those who believe that keeping the law in all its aspects, including ritual and purity laws, is essential to being a Christian. He first argues that law has an essentially educational function, that it is a schoolmaster which can be dispensed with when we come to maturity. He goes on:

> While we were minors we were enslaved to the elemental spirits of the world. But when the fullness of time had come, God sent his Son, born of a woman, born under the law, in order to redeem those who were under the law. (Gal 4.3–5)

Is the law here one of the elemental spirits from which we are freed by Christ? The balance of exegetical opinion is probably that it is not, but it is not absolutely clear, and certainly for Paul law is something from which we need to be redeemed. How can this be so? I will suggest four reasons for this.

First, we should expect a community whose story of redemption turns centrally on a political execution to have doubts about law. Perhaps Jesus did not have a 'fair trial'; perhaps there were irregularities, but it is doubtful if Rome saw it that way. Jesus' death cannot but call the morality of law into question. Furthermore, Paul urged believers not to go to law with one another (1 Cor 6). Following that advice, as we have seen, Anabaptist Christians have refused the offices of the law. They saw that the assumption of an oath is that in normal circumstances we are likely to lie and on these grounds, and on the ground of the command in Matthew 5.34–7, the Quakers refused to take the oath which, to this day, is a normal part of court process, as contrary to God's word. Suspicion of law is deep in Christianity.

Second, laws are often unjust. Augustine, followed by Aquinas, argued that unjust law was no law. We can accept this in relation to Nazi laws or apartheid laws, though we should note that the latter had the support of an avowedly Christian state, and were justified by theological argument, but the problem goes much deeper than that. Cicero quotes a popular dictum to the effect that the more law there is the less justice. He is pointing to the way legislation can actually impede the vindication of right, or can cause us to miss the wood for the trees. Further, law, we noted, emerges as society becomes more complex. Virtually all the societies we know have been class societies and those who make the law and who sentence come from the upper class and those whom they sentence from the lower class. Much law is made in their interest – sometimes egregiously, as in the eighteenth-century poaching laws. Blackstone, who codified English criminal law in the eighteenth century noted ingenuously, 'There is nothing which so generally strikes the imagination and engages the affection of mankind as the rule of property.' Even today governments are far keener to crack down on 'welfare scroungers', people who pilfer a few hundreds, than they are on corporations which filch millions. All of this calls into question the extent to which law has a truly moral claim on us. To the extent that laws do not serve the common good, to that extent they cannot genuinely claim our allegiance. As we saw in the Thirty-Nine Articles, defence of property is a key aspect of law, but we can then remind ourselves of Balzac's dictum that behind every great fortune there is a crime. To the extent that law enshrines notions of property, contractual obligation and the rights of possession as three of its principal conditions of existence, the pursuit of a purely legal equality means that law legitimizes these inequalities. Furthermore, as we have already noted, law displays a notable racial bias in most Western societies. In 1857 the US Supreme Court ruled that 'people of African descent are not and cannot be citizens of the United States and cannot sue in any court of the US' and that black people have 'no rights which whites are bound to respect'. As we shall see, black people are still quite disproportionately imprisoned on both sides of the Atlantic. We have to ask, then, whether there can be justice when the legal profession is structured to reflect and reinforce social inequality. We noted the kernel of truth in Durkheim's suggestion that the law embodies the collective consciousness, and, it could be argued, unless there were such a consciousness society could not function at all. At the same time questions of unjust power in society cannot be ignored. Is it not the case that the ruling ideas of any age, which include the making of laws, are those of the ruling class? But in that case, how can law claim to be the law of the community, and what consent can it command? The 'new criminology' of the 1970s pointed out that social contract theory was in fact an ideological framework for the protection of the rising bourgeoisie against feudal interference. It posits a consensus on the morality and permanence of the present distribution of property, characterizes all law-breaking behaviour occurring in a society where a social contract has allegedly been struck as essentially pathological or irrational, and implies that the theorists of social contract themselves had a special access to the criteria by which to judge the rationality or otherwise of an act. The whole notion of consensus sidesteps the need for ethical debate about the provisions of law (Taylor, Walton and Young, 1973).

Third, we have Paul's objection that law can only forbid and condemn sin but it cannot overcome the flesh. There is a perception here about the limits of the law's educative function. The law, Paul is saying, can coerce, but it cannot make a person moral. In considering the educative function of law we have seen that this objection is not absolute. People are formed, learn their morality, in community, and communities shape their laws. In instances already mentioned, such as legislation relating to motoring, the law has sometimes dragged an unwilling populace along behind it until its provisions were recognized as common sense. However, there is a further, more disturbing, aspect of the law and gospel debate. Lutheran thinking, up to the present, follows Augustine in distinguishing between the kingdom of God and the kingdom of this world. It argues that if the law is mistaken for the gospel the gospel loses its character as grace freely offered for all. The confusion of gospel and law leads to senti-mentalism, a tendency towards pacifism in international relations, an expectation that the state will express compassion and agape, that forgiveness should characterize the criminal justice system and that people in their secular callings should express altruism rather than self-interest. The world, it is argued, cannot be run by the gospel ethic. The world is run by law. Law is an ordinance of creation which takes account of our fallenness. It demands and coerces and judges. It does not look for perfection but goes for the best possible (Witte, 2002).

As opposed to this view we have, first, to follow Ulrich Duchrow and others in arguing that the two-kingdoms theory fatally incap-acitated the Lutheran Church in its opposition to fascism (Duchrow, 1987). The idea that the state cannot be run by the gospel ethic has in practice sanctioned colossal injustice. Second, and more funda-mentally, the opposing Calvinist position insists that God is the Lord of all life, that, as Barth put it, ruling grace is commanding grace and that the gospel itself has the form and fashion of law. There is not one law for an unredeemed and another for a redeemed world. The one word of God is both gospel and law. The law is com-pletely enclosed in the gospel. It is the claim which is addressed to us by the gospel itself and as such, because the gospel represents a claim on us, represents law. God the Judge is also the one who has mercy. The Lutheran view, then, puts apart that which God has joined together and in so doing prevents us from mounting an internal critique of the law.

Fourth, there is the popular aphorism that 'the law is an ass'. This arises because law is a clumsy instrument in dealing with the com-plexities of human behaviour. One thinks, for example, of the fishing skipper who, in order to avoid a storm, ran into harbour an hour earlier than EU law permitted and was fined £20,000, and ruined. Or the McDonald's fast-food firm taking a genuine Mrs McDonald to court because she used her name for her café in Berk-shire – and winning. Such instances are legion. The administration of the law also leaves much to be desired. A 1984 study in Britain, curtailed by the Lord Chief Justice, found that judges did not have consistent views about responding to crime, devoted little thought

to the principles on which they acted, demonstrated scant awareness of their own accumulated practice and often thought a
sentence was light when it was not, even in comparison with other
cases they had dealt with (Parker *et al.*, 1989).

In these four ways it may be argued that law is highly problematic, an ambivalent phenomenon at best, and in some cases an
instrument for class oppression. It is clear that, in the light of the
New Testament, no Christian approach to law can be other than
dialectical. One version of this dialectic appears in Augustine's
'tragic vision', mentioned in the previous chapter. We cannot do
without law, but we should not delude ourselves that it is establishing a situation which we could genuinely recognize as the human
good, as shalom. Against the tragic view, however, the alternative
account, deriving from the 'peace' churches, posits a utopian hope
which punctures complacency, which refuses to accept inequality,
injustice and class-based law as inevitable. Suspicious of law, and
even more suspicious of experts, the so-called 'princes' of law's
empire, this theological tradition nevertheless agrees that society
both can be and has to be improved, that something approaching
shalom can be realized. Another way of putting that is to say that it
aspires to the creation of a just society. What is meant by justice is
the theme of the following chapter.

3 | Social Justice and Criminal Justice

The most famous image of justice, the blindfolded figure with the uplifted sword in one hand and the scales in the other, signifies criminal justice. The scales signify the commitment to decide between guilt and innocence impartially and to weigh the evidence with as much objectivity as possible, while the sword signifies society's determination to protect itself and avenge wrongdoing. This figure, Justitia, implements the laws, and the legal system is known, in some cultures as 'the justice system'. Significantly, the Greek word for justice, *dike*, also means punishment and vengeance. Criminal justice is justice through punishment. When we identify something as a crime we assume guilt must be fixed, that the guilty must get their just deserts, that these require the infliction of pain, that justice is measured by the process and that the breaking of the law defines the offence. Establishing guilt is the hub of the whole process.

Curiously, what is meant by criminal justice often seems to have little to do with the mainstream Western discussion of justice from Plato onwards. It is also often divorced from what today is called 'social justice'. Today, as in ancient Israel, 'justice' remains a key word. In addition to criminal justice and social justice we speak of poetic justice, rough justice and natural justice. Is it possible that all these forms of justice relate to quite different things? One contemporary writer notes that 'fortunately' we can set aside the ancient discussion of justice as a virtue when discussing social justice (Miller, 1976). By contrast I shall argue that these senses are all related. In Chapter 8 I shall consider yet another construal of justice, related to these, which proposes to deal with crime primarily by dispute settlement rather than by punishment.

The most cursory glance at Aquinas' treatment of justice reveals how important the classical discussion, from Aristotle to Cicero, was for theological reflection while Plato's account was mediated to the West through Augustine. Luther himself, in a famous aside, averred that, when it came to the needs of government, 'it is my conviction that God has given and preserved such pagan books as the poets and histories, as Homer, Virgil, Demosthenes, Cicero, Livy and also that fine old lawyer Ulpian'. A few sentences later he includes Plato and Aristotle on the list, although when he is talking about theological method Aristotle is 'that rancid philosopher'. I begin my account of what is meant by criminal justice, therefore, by looking at this classical discussion.

The classical discussion

In *The Republic* Plato tries to get a fix on the nature of justice by thinking about injustice, and we should not forget that Plato's founding narrative, exactly like that of the New Testament, is one of judicial murder. In Athenian society there were many powerful individuals who threw their weight around. In material terms, and in terms of the status they enjoyed, they were highly successful individuals, but did that mean one should envy them? By no means, Plato argued. In fact it was far better to be a just person and suffer wrong or even death than to be unjust like these people, driven by greed and aggression. Trying to understand what made people greedy in this way he appealed to a medical analogy. When we are healthy, he argued, every part of our constitution is playing its proper part in relation to all the others – everything is in balance. This is how things are in the just person or state. In the unjust state or soul the different parts fail to play their proper role. Since the justice of the state depends on the justice of its rulers he saw the real answer to injustice in education. Law might restrain injustice but did not cure it. What was needed was far more radical treatment.

Plato does not often appear in discussions of criminal justice, but perhaps he should. In his own way he anticipates those thinkers who argue that the roots of crime are to be found in poor social conditioning. Of course, he makes no link between injustice and poverty, rather the opposite. In fact he would argue, as theorists of white-collar crime might argue, that poor social conditioning is more likely to be found in the households of the powerful than in the slums of the poor. Injustice, he argues, and therefore justice, has profound psychic roots, and these roots strike deep into society as a whole. He writes *The Republic* precisely because he believes that only a root-and-branch reform of society, in which power is fenced off from money, could produce a just state. Furthermore, consistently with much theory over the past two centuries, he begins with education. At this stage, before he writes *The Laws*, he is sceptical of quick fixes, including fixes by legislation. To adopt a notorious slogan, he might have said that the way to produce a better society was 'education, education, education'. Again, Plato anticipates contemporary discussion because he is quite sure there are no victimless crimes. The first person the unjust person damages, he argues, is him- or herself. Profoundly aware of the collusion between those in power and the criminal justice system Plato cannot identify justice with what happens in the courts. As a contemporary expositor of Plato, Judith Shklar, puts it, 'What do law courts do but invite the greedy to accuse the even more greedy of offences arising from greed and aggression?' (Shklar, 1990, p. 21). That is a situation which we can easily recognize in our 'culture of complaint'. Plato, then, takes us from crime to society and from society to the soul not on the grounds of an individualistic understanding of the latter but, to the contrary, on the grounds of his understanding of how the soul is shaped. The notorious discussion about banning the artists from the community is precisely about this. For 'artists' read, not Picasso or Francis Bacon, iconoclasts both, but propagandists and media tycoons. Yet again anticipating contemporary discussion Plato senses a link between the media and what we call crime.

For Plato's pupil, Aristotle, equality and proportion are the heart of his intuitions about justice. Plato had already referred to an older teacher, Simonides, who taught that justice was 'to render each his due'. This was taken up by Aristotle, was repeated by Cicero, and found its way into the jurist Ulpian and thence into European jurisprudence: *justitia est perpetua et constans voluntas suum cuique tribuendi*. Justice is a determined attempt to see that to each is given their due. This sentiment we find endlessly repeated in both the medieval and Reformation theological discussion.

As Aristotle develops the theme, justice, the heart of the virtues, is the disposition to give and receive neither too much nor too little. It differs from the other virtues in that it alone exists solely for the good of others. The word for justice, he says (appealing to a false etymology), comes from the verb to divide a line into two parts. Think of a family. It would be unjust for everyone to receive exactly equal portions at dinner because their respective needs are very different. Justice is for them to receive what they need and no more.

We can see how this applies to criminal justice in the demand that justice in sentencing means that any given offence should attract neither too much nor too little punishment, that there should not be markedly different punishments for the same crime and that the victim should be properly attended to. These are properly Aristotelian criteria for the administration of criminal justice.

Aristotle believed that reward should be apportioned according to merit but, in a view which puts sharp questions to the pattern of reward in our society, he argued that justice is a kind of mean, while injustice is excess and defect, contrary to proportion, of the useful or hurtful. Only the virtuous person, the just person, can apply these rules, and therefore make laws. The unjust person is driven by greed, and therefore breaches equality and proportionality. What the judge does is seek to restore either equality or proportion when these are breached. Justice is primarily a political virtue, found among free and equal men. The very idea of justice only makes sense within a community with a shared idea of the common good. As with Plato, it is life in the community which schools us in the meaning of justice.

Once again we see how Aristotle puts sharp questions to a society which, in its championing of difference and its moral relativism, cannot agree on an account of the common good. Such a society, Aristotle would argue, is bound to be an unjust society. It actually rules out for itself the very preconditions for knowing what justice is. Far from justice as a virtue being irrelevant to social justice such a virtue can only exist in a society where our mutual belonging in weal and woe is properly understood. To be just, on his account, is to know that no man is an island sufficient unto himself, to know that I am, at the deepest level, a community animal. Survival in the community, Aristotle implies, is only possible when each takes only what they need and makes sure that others have what they need. Indeed, to use the language of an outlandish philosophy, it is almost 'from each according to their ability to each according to their need'.

When a philosopher and political activist of an earlier generation, like Barbara Wootton, argued that in a democracy like Britain it is Parliament which decides what counts as justice, she was standing in the Aristotelian tradition. The representatives of the people argue over laws and in effect over what counts as justice. As we saw in the last chapter, this changes over time, sometimes very dramatically. What the modern tradition omits, of course, is the understanding of justice as a virtue, perhaps because the reigning individualism has lost sight of the way virtues are formed, perhaps because of the recasting of what counts as virtue under capitalism, perhaps because the dominance of utilitarianism has driven the discourse of the virtues underground for nearly two centuries. The return of virtue ethics into philosophical discussion is a welcome sign, because Aristotle's contention that justice is the very heart of the virtues, and that there can only be social justice when that is understood, remains crucial.

The Roman jurist Cicero, hugely important as one of the great teachers of the European Middle Ages, argues that passive injustice, our failure to perform our civic offices, is quite as bad as active injustice, what we would call crime. Like his Greek teachers he recognizes the priority of the common good. Justice, he argues, is the virtue that holds society together and allows us to pursue the common good for whose sake society exists. Justice alone, however, is not enough. It needs generosity to temper it. Significantly, he insists on justice for slaves, by which he means that they should be treated as waged employees.

The emphasis on passive injustice has obvious contemporary resonance. Modern Western societies, it has been argued, are characterized by such injustice, the failure to intervene whether in serious matters, like those who watched a woman in the United States being murdered, and could not even be bothered to call the police, and in trivial ones, like breaking the litter laws. Our indifference to the trivial laws signifies a cynicism which betrays the fact that we are deeply unjust societies. Justice is a whole. It cannot be broken into parts without peril. Impartiality and objectivity do not guarantee criminal justice. If we have forgotten justice as a virtue then we have forgotten justice in society, and if we have forgotten that, there can be no criminal justice either (Shklar, 1990).

Justice as a theme in Scripture

In Deuteronomy we read, 'Justice [*tsedeq*] and only justice you shall follow' (Dt 16.20), but what is this? The scriptural version of concern for the common good is, as we have seen, shalom, peace in the whole of society, or the kingdom of God. As we saw, this is not an abstract concept but is embedded in a narrative of deliverance from slavery which forms one of the two ground motifs of the biblical account of justice. The other is the idea of the covenant, the binding agreement between God and God's people which requires each party to be faithful to its provisions. It follows, in the first place, that injustice is to treat others as slaves. This, in turn, is to break the covenant, to be untrue to a particular relationship. This finds expression in the majestic words of Micah, used by the Church in the Good Friday Reproaches:

> O my people, what have I done to you?
> In what have I wearied you?
> Answer me!
> For I brought you up from the land of Egypt,
> And redeemed you from the house of slavery . . .
> With what shall I come before the LORD,
> And bow myself before God on high? . . .
> He has told you, O mortal, what is good;
> And what does the LORD require of you
> But to do justice, and to love [mercy],
> And to walk humbly with your God?
> (Mic 6.3–4, 6, 8)

As we see, the fundamental motive for love of justice is the narrative of deliverance from slavery. Because this is read as an act of unmerited love, justice is not thought of as forensic, but love and mercy are part and parcel of it. Biblical justice grows out of love. The need for justice is grounded in the righteousness and love of God. This is the fount of human justice and what is required for it, above all, is relationship with God. A later prophet spells out more precisely what such love entails:

> Is not this the fast that I choose:
>   to loose the bonds of injustice,
>   to undo the thongs of the yoke,
> to let the oppressed go free,
>   and to break every yoke?
> Is it not to share your bread with the hungry,
>   and bring the homeless poor into your house . . . ?
> Then your light shall break forth like the dawn,
>   and your healing shall spring up quickly.
> (Is 58.6–8)

In poetic form this text evokes the immense emphasis on what we would now call social justice in the Hebrew Bible. Every seven years (Deuteronomy) or every fifty years (Leviticus) debts must be remitted and families returned to their patrimony. In this way class society would be periodically deconstructed. Redistributive justice ensured a return to equality of outcome. Justice in Israel was always conceived in terms of a passionate vindication of the poor and oppressed (Ps 146.7; Dt 10.18). Nicholas Wolterstorff (1999) argues that in texts like these we hear an accent not to be encountered in the texts of Greece and Rome. It is God who, above all, does justice and this is emphasized by a constant emphasis on the needs of the poor, oppressed and marginalized. There is an obligation on all in the covenant relationship to love each one of God's creatures, each one of whom must be embraced by shalom. Against those who believe that rights discourse is foreign to Scripture, it can be argued that each person's claim on shalom establishes rights, the claim of the other on me established by the God whose primal act is deliverance from oppression. Standing in a covenant relationship with God means that, as God does justice, so we must do justice in return. To honour God is to honour the image of God, and to live in the image of God requires that we do justice. Injustice, it follows, is a form of desecration of the image and a failure to be holy even as God is holy.

Put like this it is clear how deeply Jesus' teaching in Matthew 25 is in harmony with the Hebrew Bible: the Human One is served by service of those in prison, those hungry, those in need. This is consonant, too, with Jesus' inauguration of his mission by citing Isaiah 61, and the description of what is happening to the messengers of John the Baptist in terms of the fulfilment of the messianic promises (Lk 4.18–19; 7.22–23). Jesus' practice of dining with outcasts, healing lepers and giving priority to children all instantiate the concern with peace and justice of the Hebrew Bible.

As we saw in the first chapter, translating Greek *dikaiosune* by 'justice', rather than 'righteousness', considerably changes our understanding both of Jesus and Paul. When we read that those who hunger and thirst for justice, or those who are persecuted for justice, are blessed, liberation theology suddenly seems to have more evangelical warrant. Paul's understanding of 'justification by faith' also relates to God's justice and the new social situation, shalom, which follows from that. For Paul, Christ is the justice of God, the action of God setting things to rights. Just as for Isaiah, the gospel (a very

Isaianic notion, Is 61.1) is all about God's justice, not the announcement of a bloody Assize, but of God's act and intent to create a world which conforms with God's purposes, which includes justice for the oppressed. Paul's concern for the Gentiles must be understood in line with both Jesus' concern with outcasts and the Hebrew Bible's concern with the marginalized. Justification is not, as some forms of Protestantism cast it, primarily forensic and primarily about the individual sinner but is about what God does to create justice. Its opposite is the situation where society is broken apart and fragmented, which is why Paul argues that in the new creation, 'in Christ', barriers between Jews and Gentiles, slaves and free and women and men no longer obtain.

What emerges from this account of justice is something rather different from what passes as justice in Western society. When we demand that justice is done we want to see guilt ascertained and the price paid. When Scripture speaks of justice, on the other hand, what is in view is the establishment of God's rule, of shalom. The one looks primarily to the past, the other to the future, the one is concerned primarily with retribution, the other with forgiveness and a new start, the one is excluding, and the other is including. If we take our lead from Scripture we will not be able, like so much of the contemporary discussion, to divorce questions about crime from questions of social justice.

Justice in the Christian tradition

As already noted, Christian teaching about justice involved a fusion of the classical and the biblical streams and a sort of baptism of the former. Where for Plato, for example, a person becomes just through love for the True, the Good and the Beautiful, Augustine insists that 'justice is love serving God alone'. Justice is understood as one of God's attributes or perfections. It is God's own nature which supplies the ultimate standard of justice. We know from Luther that such justice could be understood in a forensic way, as seems to have been the case with the later nominalists whom he studied, but by and large the justice of God was understood through the biblical narrative. Luther's breakthrough with regard to justification was to understand the justice of God as an expression of the mercy and forgiveness of God, as God's love seeking out the sinner for redemption. This did not mean that it ignored sin, but that it was a creative act aimed at the overcoming of sin. The disaster, with Luther, was that the two-kingdoms theory meant that this was not carried directly into the courts.

In general there seems to be a tension within Latin Christianity between this insight, which Luther re-discovers, and the difficulty of escaping from a sense of retributive justice. This sense is implicit in Anselm's argument that sin had to be paid for by the death of God's son. It is restated with great force in the distinction which Luther drew, appealing to Isaiah 28, between God's proper work of life, peace and joy, and the strange work God accomplishes by means of the law, sin, death and the devil. As a commentary on the crucifixion this is profound, but in the context of a two-kingdoms theology it can only too easily imply that retributive justice has its own proper, divinely sanctioned remit.

It was, perhaps, an unfortunate result of the manner of Luther's breakthrough that justification, which came to be one of the great watchwords of Protestantism, was understood in an exclusively individual way. It was about how God met and dealt with me as a sinner. Here Karl Barth's 1937 pamphlet, *Justification and Justice*, written in the context of National Socialism, puts the record straight. Barth insisted that the theology of justification lays on Christians the task of discerning and standing up for justice: it entails a specifically political task. It follows from the justice of God that the Christian cannot avoid the question of human rights. The Christian can only will and affirm a state which is based on justice. By any other political attitude he or she rejects the divine justification. Further, Barth insisted, a good thirty years before liberation theology emerged, that the Church must always concentrate on the poor, the socially weak and the threatened, and always stand for social justice in the political sphere. In the context of this book this means that justification also has a bearing on criminal justice – another connection which was not made by Protestantism. As we shall see in the chapter on restorative justice the gospel means nothing if it does not go beyond the forensic. Of course Barth insists, with the entire Christian tradition from Augustine onwards, that forgiveness does not condone unrighteousness. Weakness, he argues, is also a form of unrighteousness. God is merciful as God really makes demands on us and correspondingly punishes and rewards. Criminal justice, in other words, is not annulled by the gospel. In this Barth anticipates John Paul II who argues that justice constitutes the goal of forgiveness even though forgiveness does not mean indulgence towards evil. The question we have to ask is how this insight is to be worked out in relation to those we call offenders. Here Barth's own practice has something to teach us for when the Swiss popular press started an anti-Nazi witch-hunt in 1945 (having carefully sat on the fence for the first three years of the war) Barth insisted that Christ called even the SS and the Gestapo to repentance. Justice is essentially relational and can best be exemplified in a community of restored relationships and healed memories.

On the Catholic side Aquinas took from Aristotle the understanding of justice as a virtue. Justice is, as Augustine said, the love of God and our neighbour pervading all the other virtues. If we ask what the Christian tradition adds to Aristotle it seems to be two things: first, Aquinas argues that works of mercy and compassion are proper outworkings of justice. Second, where for Aristotle we learn justice through the civic community, for Aquinas it is the Church which schools us in the virtues, and we thus learn justice from the whole biblical story and through the liturgy. That the eucharist schools us in our understanding of justice means that liturgical reform is not a trivial matter. As argued in the first chapter, the Book of Common Prayer instils a deeply retributive approach to criminal justice. Behind some of the alternative liturgies, in *Common Worship* for example, lies a quite different understanding of society and therefore of criminals and of how we deal with them. Here, by a nice ecumenical irony, it is the Methodist Stanley Hauerwas who most advances our understanding of this insight, insisting that the Church does not *have* a social ethic but *is* a social ethic. For the Church to act justly is for it to be the servant community and to manifest the peaceable kingdom in the world.

Reflecting on Aristotle's version of *suum cuique* (to each his own), Aquinas articulated an extremely important discussion of economic justice in terms of the just wage and the just price. The attempt to see that people were properly rewarded for their labour, and that prices should not be either depressed or inflated was an important anticipation of what later came to be called social justice.

The past thirty years have seen a renewed interest in virtue ethics, and the correlative insistence that virtues are only acquired in community. Our understanding of justice will be fundamentally shaped by the foundation story of our community – which is why the current dominance of the story of the 'free market' as the meaning of 'freedom' is so worrying. The Christian story, on the other hand, looks back to God's care for the oppressed lived out in Christ, exemplified in his death, understood as justifying the whole of sinful humankind. That last phrase is not a pious sentiment, as we shall see in the next chapter, for, as Barth insisted in a notable sermon, it brings the respectable in their pews or holy huddles into line with the criminals in our jails. Justification, properly understood, has real implications for criminal justice. So too, however, has the priority of the poor.

Social justice

It is sometimes argued that the notion of social justice is peculiarly modern. As a matter of terminology this may be correct but, as we have seen, what is called social justice is a central concern of both the Hebrew Bible and of some parts of the Christian tradition. Social justice is defined, using economic terminology, as the question of the distribution of benefits and burdens throughout a society in terms of all major human goods such as housing, health, education and so forth. If we begin from the prophets, the question of social justice is the question of how we reconcile beliefs in human equality, on the one hand, with the facts of poverty and wealth, manifest social disparities, on the other. One of the most contentious and influential accounts of this theme comes from the Austrian philosopher Friedrich Hayek in his book *The Mirage of Social Justice*. Hayek argues that the accounts of justice which we have so far reviewed are all very well for small societies where everyone knows everyone. In a market society, however, they are simply irrelevant. Market societies work by the operation of an invisible hand, as Adam Smith argued, co-ordinating millions of decisions to buy with prices and therefore wages. In such a society questions of justice just do not arise. Or rather, perhaps, the market itself, blindfolded if not committed to objectivity, is in itself the new image of justice. Great poverty, and the suffering that attends it, may be regrettable but it is the price we pay for progress for, it is argued, it is the market which has been the driving force behind the immense technological advances humankind has achieved over the past two hundred years, which have lightened the burden of human toil and suffering as no other system has or could. In this system the allocation of wealth and property can be neither just nor unjust, because such language implies it to be the result of an act of will but in fact the results are not intended or foreseen and depend on a multitude of circumstances not known in their totality to anybody. For Hayek strangers have no moral claim on us and there is no form of human solidarity which implies that we should help and sustain one another. It might be objected that this is the ethical attitude which allowed the Holocaust to take place, as Daniel Goldhagen has argued. However, the dark other in Hayek's account is Soviet communism, the attempt to produce a just society by regulation and compulsion. It deprives us of choice which is at the heart of Hayek's view of what it means to be human. Freedom is the heart of human dignity, and freedom means choice, and choice implies an absence of regulation. The social Welfare State, which tries to redistribute wealth from rich to poor, to see that the shares of the cake allocated to all are less unequal than they might be, is not only misguided, sapping of moral fibre for the poor, but also morally wrong. It has simply misunderstood what it means to be human.

This argument does not question the realities which follow from class societies. The 1994 *Report of the Commission on Social Justice* in Britain noted that those who live in the most affluent areas can expect to live eight years longer than those in the most deprived areas; that the attempted suicide rate for unemployed men is between ten and fifteen times higher than among men in work; and the top 10 per cent of households pay 32 per cent of their income in tax, compared to 43 per cent for the bottom 10 per cent. Many other reports have repeatedly found that all over the world all the major killer diseases affect the poor more than the rich; that the poor are less healthy, die younger and have a higher incidence of both mental disorder and physical illness than the rich. Further, the gap between rich and poor within the Northern countries, which is greater than at any time since 1886, is mirrored and writ large in the relation between Northern and Southern countries, which form effectively a kind of international underclass. As we shall see in the next chapter these facts are directly correlated with statistics on crime and punishment, even if the nature of the correlation is not agreed. All around the world it is the poor, the disturbed and the disadvantaged who are over-penalized and over-imprisoned. Whatever the exact nature of the causality there is no question that societies with high levels of inequality and marginalization tend to be high-crime societies and it is also true that a system which singles out the

poor and by its actions harms their children can hardly be considered a system of justice.

Such facts raise grave problems for Christians on four counts. In
the first place, when the eighth-century prophets are read as part of
God's command, their critique of prevailing injustice in their
society, of the gap between rich and poor, of luxury on the one hand
and indigence on the other, reads like a description of the results of
a class society. This was indeed how Christian socialists read such
texts. Hayek's pronouncement that the arrival of the 'free' market
has changed the moral foundations of society was not open to those
for whom such texts were in some sense 'the Word of God'. On the
contrary, they read such texts as a command to do something about
such facts, to change them. There were, of course, fellow Christians
who argued that the best way to do that was to let the market have
its way but to continue or increase charitable provision for the poor,
but this seemed a poor account of the prophetic demand for justice
to roll down like waters.

In the second place, Christian theologians have taken over
Cicero's concern for passive injustice, which sounds very much like
the attitude of those on the left hand in Jesus' parable of the sheep
and the goats. In our society the operations of the market render
those in prison, hungry or naked invisible. The implication of the
parable is that if we see suffering and fail to do anything about it
that is in fact unjust, it fails to heed God's command to be our
brother's keeper. Such a point should alert us to the fundamental
incompatibility between Hayek's system and the gospel. Hitler, we
know, had an ultimate goal of destroying Christianity altogether,
and replacing it with a new paganism. The gospel of National Socialism and the gospel of Jesus Christ were fundamentally incompatible. This other incompatibility, between a system which cannot by
definition see the needs of the other and a system which is required
to prioritize the needs of the other, is not so often remarked.

In the third place there is a challenge from the Christian reading
of *suum cuique*. What does it mean for each to be given their due if
each human being is a sister or brother of the Human One (which is
the Christian gloss on being created in the image of God)? Why
does exploitation matter? Why do we feel outraged by stories of
children in Asia sewing footballs for a few pence a day? The answer
lies in our understanding of what it means to be human. What is
outraged is an intrinsic dignity which in turn calls for a basic

equality of treatment between persons. The eucharist adumbrates as a sign the view that the world is gifted to all creatures and is to be shared equally between them. Equality as God's creature demands equality of resource allocation. We can follow up this probing of the implications of *suum cuique* by considering what have been argued to be the main aspects of any account of social justice, namely an understanding of rights, deserts and needs (Miller, 1976).

Some theologians consider the discourse of rights to be antithetical to the gospel. This is against a background where everyone's claiming of rights can be a manifest form of selfishness. I argued in the previous chapter, however, that rights do indeed follow from the gospel in the sense that there are things which follow necessarily from our being in the image of God. Negatively this precludes the use of torture, or 'cruel and unusual punishments'. Positively it includes all the basic goods outlined by the 1948 Declaration of Human Rights. Far from these being antithetical to the gospel they are included in it. Of course, this constitutes a moral right rather than a legal one, but again, on the account of law in the previous chapter, moral rights need to be worked out in legal terms.

The language of deserts is more problematic for the theologians. It is strongly counter-intuitive that an idle scoundrel should get the same reward as someone who works hard. Paul, as we know, gave short shrift to people who claimed this: 'If any one will not work, neither shall he eat' (2 Thess 3.10 NKJV). He could appeal to the famous advice of the Wisdom writers: 'Go to the ant, thou sluggard; consider her ways and be wise' (Prov 6.6 AV). This attitude, however, was problematized by Jesus in the parable of the eleventh-hour labourers, which John Ruskin used as the basis for his polemical pamphlet on economics, *Unto this Last*. The Protestant work ethic does not seem to be grounded in the gospel, according to which we are all unworthy servants, all members one of another, all radically dependent on grace. On these grounds we can say that the Christian gospel is incompatible with meritocracy. If "'tis mercy all', and all is grace, then there are no just deserts but only unmerited gift, although this was never understood to be a license for idleness or loose behaviour, which is the point of Paul's warning in Thessalonians.

This point about deserts overlaps with the point about needs. Of course we live in a world of rising expectations where 'needs' are constantly redefined. There is a temptation, on the part of right-wing thinkers, to pare them down to simple subsistence, and on the part of others to so define them in terms of relative deprivation that failure to possess a car, television and mobile phone is a sign of unmet need. Both extremes should be avoided. The UN Declaration, once again, gives its account of rights in terms of basic goods of shelter, health, food and education which are essential to human flourishing, sometimes called intrinsic needs. There certainly are issues of relative provision here which are important, but the context is global and we are far from a situation where the basic needs of all those made in the image are met, which is the fundamental demand of the Christian gospel.

This leads to the fourth point which is that, as I argued in the first chapter, community is at the heart of the gospel. On the scriptural understanding we are all members one of another. It is for this reason that we can only have a rational and humane penal policy 'if crime is accepted as a social phenomenon, a problem of communities as a whole rather than of individual bad apples, and as a communal duty rather than appertaining solely to formal law enforcement and criminal justice agencies' (Hudson, 1993, p. 174). Concretely this means that the imperative to improve the criminal justice system is not just a matter of the judiciary learning a little sociological common sense, improving prison regimes, increasing the use of probation, devising more realistic schemes of rehabilitation, essential as all those things are, but, more fundamentally, recovering the sense of community, of shared weal and woe.

In the past thirty years the text which has provoked most discussion of justice in general and social justice in particular is John Rawls' *A Theory of Justice*. Let us imagine, he proposes, that we could begin with a clean slate and construct a society just as we wanted. We would do so in such a way that, first, every person had an equal right to the most extensive basic liberty compatible with a similar liberty for others, and, second, so that the inequalities which we know are bound to arise from unequal gifts are so arranged that they are to the benefit of the least advantaged and attached to offices and positions open to all under conditions of fair equality of opportunity. What ensures fairness of distribution are fair methods and procedures, for there are no absolute criteria to appeal to. With Aristotle he recognizes that equality does not mean that everyone receives the same: it would be absurd to insist that someone who was seriously disabled had exactly the same needs as an able-bodied person.

The poll tax imposed by the Thatcher government came adrift on precisely this principle. Rawls believes that this idea corresponds to the basic ethical intuitions of social democracies, what he calls an 'overlapping consensus'. Although Rawls' framework is basically individualistic he recognizes some form of the common good in the argument that, since we do not deserve the talents we are born with, society has a right to redistribute the benefits we accrue by them. Like the classical theories, Rawls too has a political model in the background, in this case the idea of the social contract.

Rawls' theory has attracted much Christian critique. For Rawls justice is fairness but, say his Christian critics, fairness is not enough. Rawls misses the passion for justice of the Christian Scriptures and offers us a fundamentally individualist account of justice which fails to understand the importance of community and the story that community lives by. This failure damages our understanding of what it means to be a person. Neither does he have any answer to the problems raised by vested power. He believes that justice can be had without sacrifice, but this is impossible (Forrester, 1997).

For all his concern for fairness his account of pure procedural justice is actually an endorsement of the invisible hand and this seems to be at odds with his desire to see that the most disadvantaged benefit from the distribution of goods. What would seem to follow from this, rather than simple market allocation, would be some version of redistributive economy.

Shalom and the call to justice

Justice, the Christian tradition has wanted to say, is one of the attributes or perfections of God. The divine justice, as this is attested in Scripture, is an active and passionate creation of and demand for shalom, for a situation in which the proper dignity and requirements of all creatures is respected. Shalom is all-embracing: the interrelation of individual and community and of community and environment is included in it. When the Christian tradition followed Plato and Aristotle and spoke of justice as a virtue they understood justice as a matter of being conformed to the God who is justice in Godself. Such conformity disallows the divisions of justice suggested by some philosophers, between social justice and criminal justice, and between these forms of justice and the justice of the soul. Perhaps one cannot say that justice is whole or it is nothing. The Augustinian vision I outlined in the first chapter acknowledges the partial and fragmentary character of what we call 'justice' in our polities. On the other hand any complacency about injustice is equally forbidden by the divine justice we have to follow. It is significant that in the New Testament the structures of society are spoken of in terms of the 'principalities and powers' which, according to the author of Ephesians, crucified Christ. The abstractness of Rawls' account belies the fact that there is a 'domination system' formed by assumptions about what is and is not possible, and about what counts as value. The Hebrew prophets, and their Christian successors, have addressed that domination system with impassioned advocacy. The blindfolded figure of justice was a common figure on the facades of the great medieval cathedrals, but perhaps their sculptors had not studied their texts closely enough. The justice which brings social, economic and criminal justice together is the figure of the Hebrew judge, smiting the oppressor, standing up for the poor:

> Give justice to the weak and the orphan;
>> maintain the right of the lowly and the destitute.
> Rescue the weak and the needy;
>> deliver them from the hand of the wicked.
>>>> (Ps 82.3–4)

The person who does this is the virtuous person who necessarily stands for and works for social justice. The welfare consensus of the 1940s was, I have argued, a partial and limited, but nevertheless true and concrete, instantiation of shalom. In many ways and for many reasons that has run into the sand, and political programmes intended to rethink response to need are certainly necessary. Unfortunately what has happened is that such programmes have begun from the assumption that the market is the best means of provision and, as we have seen, such an assumption sidelines the whole question of justice as understood from Scripture and tradition. At the same time it problematizes the very possibility of criminal justice. Market societies talk endlessly of the war on crime, but have they a moral right to do so? It is to the question of crime, then, that I now turn.

4 | Crime and Responsibility

Every Christmas when English-speaking Christians sing the carol *In Dulci Jubilo* they come across the line, 'Deeply were we stained *per nostra crimina*'. The Latin word *crimen* means charge, accusation, reproach, fault, guilt, scandal. It is, of course, the word from which we derive our word 'crime'. In the carol it obviously means 'sin'. How are they related? 'If a man commits adultery with the wife of his neighbour, both the adulterer and the adulteress shall be put to death' (Lev 20.10). This is an example of something which, in post-exilic Israel, seems to have been both a sin and a crime but in present-day Western society remains a sin but is no longer a crime. In some Muslim societies, as we know, it remains both. On the positivist view, as we saw in Chapter 2, a crime is technically nothing more than a breach of the law of a community. Suspicious of moral categories, positivists still had to invoke them when giving an account of why some forms of behaviour were proscribed. 'Do this because I say so!' is not an adequate response even for children. In common parlance people often conflate sin and crime, even at a sophisticated level. Thus the former Master of the Rolls in Britain, Lord Denning, wrote: 'In order that an act should be punishable it must be morally blameworthy. A certain kind of immorality should be a necessary, though not sufficient condition of criminality. It must be a sin.' Turning that around, the theologian Hastings Rashdall wrote: 'A crime is a sin it is expedient to repress by penal enactment.' This seems to be saying that some sins so affect the wider community that they have to be proscribed by law, and thereby become crimes, while other sins may be the target of disapprobation but are not penalized. But of course unjust states may criminalize moral forms of behaviour, as eighteenth-century England criminalized ancient traditions of using the commons, or apartheid South Africa criminalized mixed-race marriages, while society may sanction and even reward forms of behaviour which many might consider sinful and might perhaps want criminalized, such as some forms of financial trading, arms trading and gambling. The gap between sin and crime which these distinctions indicate can also be seen by the fact that while, according to Scripture, all humans are sinful, only a tiny percentage come through the criminal justice system. The relation between sin and crime, therefore, is not one of identity, but common issues are involved in both. While there are many societies which do not work with sin as a category, there are no societies for which 'anything goes'. Rather, as argued in Chapter 2, society is constituted by drawing boundaries which ought not to be transgressed, by defining behaviour which is, or is not, acceptable. Both 'sin' and 'crime' describe patterns of behaviour which damage human society, and therefore the possibility of being human, to varying extents, and which therefore constitute boundaries. We could say 'crime' is the legal definition of such behaviour, and 'sin' the theological. This is true but not very illuminating. In attempting to explore the relationship I shall first consider the nature of sin, and then turn to various ways of understanding crime before returning to the issue of sin, crime and human nature.

Sin

The word 'sin' is, strictly speaking, a theological word, referring human behaviour to God as its ultimate criterion. 'Against thee only have I sinned, and done this evil in thy sight,' says the psalmist (Ps 51.4, BCP). For the atheist there can be crimes, and injustice, but no sins. For the believer, on the other hand, 'Whatever does not proceed from faith is sin' (Rom 14.23). One of the most important words translated 'sin' in the Hebrew Bible, *pesah*, means rebellion, active turning away from God. Sin is expressed in acts of transgression, particular sins, but refers fundamentally to the relationship between God and humankind which has been broken by unfaithfulness (Hos 4.1; 6.7; Is 1.2; Jer 4.17). When the Church talks of sin, therefore, it is not just talking about wrongdoing but making a claim about the source of that wrongdoing. It claims that to be truly human we have to be in relationship with God, conform to God, and that if that is not the case we are bound to sin. This in turn means that Denning and Rashdall's easy conflation of sin and crime is not strictly speaking accurate.

Christian theology has reflected in a number of ways on the understanding of sin as rebellion. In the tradition from at least the fourth century, pride has been seen as the paradigm form of sin, the conviction that it is possible to live without God. Milton's Satan is the classic instance here:

> I 'sdain'd subjection, and thought one step higher
> Would set me highest, and in a moment quit
> The debt immense of endless gratitude,
> So burdensome, still paying, still to owe;
> Forgetful what from him I still received.
> (*Paradise Lost*, Book IV)

Milton here expresses Anselm's understanding of sin as failing to pay God God's due. Anselm went further, drawing on a social world-view where offence was relative to the status of the one offended, to argue that the smallest offence against God was infinite, because God was an infinite being. But what constitutes an offence against God? Blackstone, the eighteenth-century jurist, begins his list of possible crimes with offences against God and religion. Blasphemy, then, was a sin peculiarly directed against God. But, drawing on the deepest insights of the New Testament, blasphemy does not outrage God but the feelings of the community, and if people are executed or murdered on account of it then God is reduced to the level of a fetish. People are sacrificed to the deified solidarity of the community. Our deepest insight into what constitutes an offence against God comes, as we would expect, in the teaching of Jesus, and especially in the story of the sheep and the goats in Matthew 25. This highlights the way in which attitudes to God, positive and negative, find practical expression in the way in which all fellow humans are treated (beginning with the outcasts rather than with 'VIPs'). An offence against the image of God, even if it is the result of passive injustice, is an offence against God. If we begin here we are less inclined to make pride and unbelief the paradigm sin and we are also able to make more sense of the equivalence of sin and crime. 'Sin' on this account might be failure to live in a fully reciprocal, caring way which is in turn a failure to recognize the image of God in everyone. In turn, we might want to say, it is proper to deal with some forms of such behaviour by penal enactment.

Another important word for sin in Hebrew is *chattah*, or Greek *hamartia*. Both words mean at root 'missing the mark', a metaphor from archery. Humans ought to do this, to live in accordance with God's will, but in fact they do that. The Hebrew Bible draws attention to violence and murder, adultery, theft, coveting, oppression and extortion, deceit, fraud and lying as instances of 'sin'. Why? What is intrinsically wrong with them? They breach the covenant between God and the community, a covenant which expresses what is believed to be the secret of human flourishing, the clue to life in all its fullness. Such acts destroy community and thereby the very possibility of constructive human life, the heart of the divine project. For this reason Amos castigates the nations for what today we would call 'crimes against humanity' (Amos 1 and 2). The whole prophetic denunciation of injustice rests on the assumption that God has shown what is good – to do justice, love mercy and walk humbly with God. Failure to walk on this narrow path is sin, which is not a piece of priestly ideology but a sober assessment of what makes for life.

Against this the Enlightenment critic can object that much which appears in the law codes of the Hebrew Bible is far from life-giving. Are you really saying, they can ask, that people ought to be stoned for gathering firewood on the Sabbath (Num 15) or for that matter for homosexuality or adultery? To raise such questions is to point to the ongoing debate as to what 'missing the mark' actually entails. The Church believes that what it means to be truly human is revealed in Jesus, but not as a blueprint, a set of codes, perhaps 613 commandments, which can be followed to give the desired result. Paul's polemic against the law was directed at just such an attitude, as was Jesus' argument about the true meaning of the Sabbath.

In the Hebrew Scriptures we find an argument about the effect of sin from one generation to another. The early saying that the children pay for the sins of the fathers (Jer 31.29) represents the perception that destructive behaviour sets up a pattern of consequences which repeats itself and becomes part of the structure of society. In the exilic and post-exilic writings, especially Ezekiel, we find a contrary insistence that 'the soul that sins shall die' and that sin does not apply to the whole community (Ezek 18). In this respect the earlier view of both the prophets and Deuteronomy that, to use Schleiermacher's phrase, 'sin is in each the work of all and in all the work of each', seems more realistic. Texts (for example 1 Kings 8.46 or Rom 3.10) which were later taken to assert the universality of sin represent a realistic recognition of the impossibility of stepping outside of society. The North African theology of Tertullian and Augustine developed this insight into the doctrine of original sin. Although this sometimes found bizarre forms of expression, at root it expresses a very profound insight about what it means to be human, namely that we are all formed and conditioned by warped patterns of relating which go back to the very dawn of humanity and that these warped patterns mean that we are bound to sin. This has far-reaching implications for criminal justice. Augustine, Luther and Calvin, and indeed the Western tradition as a whole, all speak of a bondage of the will while at the same time insisting that we are responsible for our actions. This paradoxical claim represents a tightrope which both theology and criminal justice have to walk. On the one hand, the idea of a free will which can choose just what it wants to do, whether deriving from Pelagius or from the Enlightenment, is a fantasy. All of us are shaped by our genetic and social inheritance, by our implication in the sin of humanity, and indeed sometimes by sheer bad luck, which may lead people to crime. Thomas Hardy's *Tess of the D'Urbervilles*, subtitled 'A Pure Woman', with its sub-plot of unsympathetic evangelicals, with their (very Pelagian) insistence on every individual's ability to choose, is designed to make just this point. On the other hand we have to insist on human responsibility, because without that human dignity is compromised and we are all reduced to the status of patients with some kind of mental disorder, pleading 'diminished responsibility'. In order to be convicted in court *mens rea* has to be established, by which is meant that a crime is committed knowingly and wantonly, that it is a deliberate wicked act. This assumes that we do indeed retain some freedom to act, a point Paul insists on in relation to the Gentiles (Rom 1.20).

The issue of freedom versus bondage of the will is extremely vexed, as Milton, once again, notes, depicting some of the infernal angels' reasoning:

> Of Providence, Foreknowledge, Will and Fate,
> Fixt Fate, free Will, Foreknowledge absolute,
> And found no end, in wandring mazes lost.
> Of good and evil much they argu'd then,
> Of happiness and final misery,
> Passion and Apathie, and glory and shame,
> Vain wisdom all, and false Philosophie.
>
> (*Paradise Lost*, Book II)

One hears in this passage Milton's frustrated response to a thousand debates in which he has taken part or to which he has been a listener. Those theologians who have emphasized the bondage of the will most strenuously have generally done so alongside a conviction of the *praedestinatio gemina*, the twofold predestination to damnation or salvation. To do so is to invite theological sophistry in the attempt, at the same time, to maintain human freedom and therefore the responsibility for our actions. One can see how such sophistry is arrived at for we have no option but to affirm a dialectic of freedom and bondage. On the one hand the idea that we might be free in the sense of being completely unconstrained in our actions, unrestricted and unconditioned, stands up to no kind of scrutiny. The doctrine of bondage to sin very properly made this point. On the other hand without freedom there is no morality and no love, and the human story becomes meaningless. The Church correctly insists that the gospel is not about morality but what it means by this is not that moral actions do not count, but that for actions to be truly moral they need to be rooted in the love of God, in grace. But where does such a claim leave criminal justice, which does not operate in the theological but in the secular realm? Given bondage of the will, is *mens rea* a legitimate assumption? Against the Augustinian position that 'the best virtues of good pagans are nothing but splendid vices' I set the Calvinist, or perhaps better, Barthian insistence that Christ rules in the midst of his enemies. The image of God, and therefore the possession of something which may meaningfully be called freedom, is not obliterated by sin. If it were, there could be no moral or theological justification for criminal justice whatsoever. What is needed is a distinction between partial and complete freedom. Freedom, we know, can be construed positively or negatively, as freedom from or freedom for. None of us are free in the sense of being unconstrained. True freedom, however, consists in the enlargement of our faculties, in the furtherance of our ability to love, in the extension of our humanity. The love of God which holds all things in being sees to it that that freedom is never reduced to vanishing point. It is failure to see that which accounts for the sour taste of Augustine's anti-Pelagian treatises. Human beings are in bondage, but they also have some freedom. The gospel meets them with a claim that true freedom is to be found in the service of God, that the real furthering of our ability to love is only found there. This claim goes way beyond the minimal assumptions of criminal justice. What remains contentious is the degree of responsibility we can allow to human actions. This is a crucial issue when it comes to so-called 'crimes of attempt', the most famous of which, in British history, is the attempt by Guy Fawkes and his fellow conspirators to blow up the House of Commons. No offence was committed but Fawkes was nevertheless tried, found guilty and hung, drawn and quartered. In an attempt, intent or will is the principal ingredient of the crime and, as in the Gunpowder Plot, such attempts may be sentenced as severely as completed acts. The debate around criminal attempts, divided between subjectivists, who concentrate on the intention, and objectivists, who concentrate on what was actually committed, focuses attention precisely on the relation between crime and the will. To what extent can I be said to be constrained by others or by my situation? Are there those who, like Dostoevsky's Idiot, may have radical ideas but are intrinsically harmless and should thus be judged incapable of doing serious harm?

Some theologians seek to turn the inevitability of the dialectic of freedom and bondage by understanding evolution as a process in the course of which one animal species is being hominized, and in which moral conscience slowly unfolds from the tangle of instincts and determinations. 'Sin', then, is no moral absolute, but a marker of where we are on the evolutionary course. Others point out that the transition from hunter-gatherer to more complex societies involved what we now see as immature adjustments, which deal with opposition through separation, denial and repression. On this understanding salvation is the attainment of greater maturity and the enabling of less repressive styles of life. Non-Christian religions put the question to us of whether we need a concept of sin at all. Given their framework of karma, the working out of good and bad deeds in a previous life, both Hinduism and Buddhism manage without one. It can be argued that the notion of what it is to be a person in Hinduism is indeed very different from that in the West and this might pose interesting problems for Indian jurisprudence. However this might be, it seems that we cannot eliminate the notion of sin and responsibility because, as I have argued, without responsibility not only would there be no criminal justice system but we would live in a sub-moral world in which the very notion of person would no longer be possible and love would not be part of the vocabulary. Both theology and criminal justice, therefore, have no option but to embrace the dialectic of bondage and responsibility. I turn now to a discussion of the nature of crime.

Types of crime

Broadly speaking it is helpful to follow the alliterative, though rough, distinction between street crime, suite crime and state crime. When politicians talk of the 'war on crime' or 'being tough on crime'; when television stations aim for guaranteed viewing ratings with cops and robbers series; when bookstores have a section called 'crime fiction'; when the British Crime Survey or the American Crime Index appear each year with statistics showing simultaneously a rise and a decline in crime, what they are talking about in each case is so-called street crime. Blackstone, in his famous compendium of criminal law in Britain written in the eighteenth century, distinguishes between offences against God and religion; against the state; against the person; and against property. Today in Britain there are more than one hundred different categories of notifiable offence. However, the British Crime Survey distinguishes broadly between property crime and violence, though drug offences, handling stolen goods, fraud, forgery and criminal damage do not really fit comfortably into either pigeonhole. Currently in Britain, burglary, car theft and vandalism are the main forms of property crime, though thefts of mobile phones have also reached sensational proportions in recent years.

Most assaults in contemporary Britain are domestic violence and most are against women. Street assaults are nearly as common, and most involve men. Violent offences make up a quarter of all known offences and 'serious' assaults usually only involve minor injury. Although domestic violence is found in every sector of the population crimes of violence are most often committed in poor neighbourhoods. There has been a steep rise in street crime in most societies, outside Japan, in the past fifty years. Some crimes, such as shoplifting, are under-reported.

Street crime is overwhelmingly the crime of the urban poor, who in every country form the bulk of the prison population. It shades off into organized crime, by which is meant activities such as drug-peddling, extortion, kidnapping for profit, illegal toxic waste dumping, credit card fraud, smuggling, intellectual theft, and corruption. In this kind of crime those at the top may be substantial and even respectable citizens, while those who carry out criminal operations on the ground will generally be the urban poor. Studies of criminal markets have indicated that there is not the clear distinction which one might imagine between these kinds of activity, on the one hand, and respectable business and even the work of the state on the other.

Suite crime is crime committed by big business and is known variously as 'white-collar crime', 'corporate crime' or 'crimes of the powerful'. Ever since Sutherland's famous account of white-collar crime in 1948 criminologists have emphasized that this kind of crime is both widespread and far more serious in its impacts than street crime. Despite this, suite crime continues to attract far less attention from governments, law-makers and the media for a variety of reasons. Sometimes the details are hard to follow, it certainly lends itself far less to dramatization and, most seriously, it rests on assumptions and practices which are shared by the powerful groups in society as a whole, including politicians and judges. Much white-collar crime is simply regarded as an extension of the privileges of white-collar status. Enron engaged in what the press refers to as 'creative accounting' and its former CEO still strenuously denies he did anything wrong.

Suite crime may embrace many types of behaviour. A North American study in 1980 distinguished between administrative violations, such as failure to comply with legal requirements; environmental violations; financial violations, including illegal payments and tax violations; labour violations, including health and safety issues; manufacturing violations, mainly related to product safety; and unfair trade practices (Clinard and Yeager, 1980). The list of notorious cases is breathtaking and includes the decision of the Ford Motor Company to go ahead with production of its Pinto model, even when it was known to be dangerous, because it was calculated that it was cheaper to pay damages than to withdraw the model, a decision which resulted in the death by fire of between five and nine hundred people and thousands being scarred for life; the *Herald of Free Enterprise* disaster, in which 192 people died; Bhopal, in which more than four thousand died; the marketing of the Dalkon Shield contraceptive on the basis of falsified test results, which led to death, infertility and illness; the collapse of Barings and of Enron; the Maxwell Pension Fund scandal; the Piper Alpha explosion which killed 167 offshore workers; and, more recently, a number of train crashes on the British rail network. The cost/benefit calculations made by Ford in the Pinto case actually came to light, but were nothing new. Right at the beginning of the twentieth century Max Weber had observed that the Chicago tramway company had calculated that it was cheaper to pay out regular sums for death and injury than to upgrade the tramway. Braithwaite (1984) found in a study of the pharmaceutical industry that bribery was commonplace, that there was frequently negligent safety-testing of drugs, that legal drugs were illicitly promoted and that out-of-date or dangerous drugs were dumped on the Third World, or the Third World was used as a testing ground for them. There were also numerous forms of financial irregularities including fraud and transfer pricing. Nineteen of the twenty largest pharmaceutical companies have disclosed foreign bribes to the Securities and Exchange Commission. The Fortune 500 firms averaged one violation apiece of antitrust laws in 1984. Braithwaite therefore concludes that most major corporations are recidivist law-breakers.

The sums of money involved in suite crime, when they can be estimated with any accuracy, consistently prove to dwarf the sums involved in street crime. In 1985 in Britain the total cost of fraud reported to fraud squads amounted to £213 million, which was twice the cost of theft, burglary and robbery reported in that year. Twelve years later the average amount taken in a burglary was £370, while the Serious Fraud Office reckoned in any one year to investigate between 39 and 82 cases, the aggregate value of which was between £1.2 billion and 'in excess of £5 billion'. Tens of millions of pounds are thought to be lost each year by prescription frauds and false claims of payment by dentists, doctors, pharmacists and opticians. Mis-selling of pensions involves perhaps £11 billion, or more. In the United States corporate tax fraud is estimated to cost between $7 billion and $50 billion annually. Quite apart from fraud, businessmen and women or large corporations can avoid breaking the letter of the law, while flouting its spirit, by employing expert advice.

Suite crime also involves huge numbers of injuries and even deaths. Slapper and Tombs (1999) calculate that for one year in Britain, 1994, when the Health and Safety Executive acknowledged 376 fatal injuries, the proper figure for occupationally caused fatal illnesses and deaths from fatal injuries was 3,018. Trades unions calculated that more than ten thousand people per year died from work-related medical conditions. These figures did not include deaths from asbestos. At this time there was an average of 834 murders per year. Slapper and Tombs conclude that many corporate crimes 'have enormous physical consequences: unsafe pharmaceutical products, illegal emissions into the environment, unsafe working conditions, unfit food products, and so on, kill, maim and render sick, both chronically and acutely, thousands of citizens' (Slapper and Tombs, 1999, p. 79). Since these consequences fall largely on the poor they also conclude that corporate crimes have pernicious and destructive social effects.

In all these cases the question of establishing corporate responsibility has proved exceptionally difficult. Corporations are complex, lines of responsibility dense, records are easy to doctor or to shred, and so forth. In the case of Bhopal, for example, Union Carbide laid the responsibility on its Indian managers, while in the case of Piper Alpha Shell took out an injunction against being sued in a US court. In the Pinto case Ford argued successfully that car manufacturers could not be held responsible for dangerous driving.

The prevalence of corporate crime can lead to the conclusion that capitalism is criminogenic, in promoting competitive behaviour which puts ends before means. When the Equity Insurance Group wrote up thousands of fake insurance policies this was, it has been argued, not an aberration but a logical outcome of the morality of the New York Stock Exchange. It is also the case that, since the law has been framed both within a capitalist environment and by the ruling class, it sanctions many activities which, in moral terms, are distinctly questionable. In the Barings case, had Nick Leeson's bet on futures succeeded, as many of his earlier bets had done, he would have been applauded as one of the most gifted operators on the financial markets. George Soros caused a major devaluation of sterling by betting on the pound, which in turn led to rises in unemployment and all the consequences in terms of broken homes, rises in street crime and suicide which follow from that, but no one suggests he should be locked up. Negligence, failure to maintain safe working conditions, adequate safety standards and so forth are not criminalized, though in common parlance we might say 'It's a crime!' The difference between the approach to street crime and suite crime is illustrated by the way the two are treated: misrepresentation in advertisements is a breach of a code, not a crime; claiming extra benefits is a crime, but not finding tax loopholes; pilfering is a crime, but not overcharging nationalized industries; physical assault is, rightly, a crime, but not making people work in a polluted environment.

Although white-collar crime costs the community more, and is often more serious in its effects than street crime, it is dealt with in a different way, often by regulation, which does not on the whole use the sanctions of the criminal law to secure compliance. This fact calls into question the rhetoric of the war on crime, and the soaring rates of imprisonment which we will consider in Chapter 6, and invites us to reflect on the way in which crime is theorized. The priority of street crime on the political agenda of most countries raises important questions about our understanding of the common good, about shalom. We know, for example, that children are far more at risk from motor traffic than they are from paedophiles, but newspapers mount no campaigns against those who break the 30 mph speed restriction, in fact virtually the entire community does it routinely. The obsession with street crime seems to preclude a proper discussion of the common good. We have to ask whether breaking and entering or using overseas tax havens is a more serious abuse of the community. For one you may end up in prison, the other is consistent with holding high public office. When it comes to punishment, however, someone must show that crime doesn't pay, and we know who: social classes four and five.

State crime is even more problematic than white-collar crime. Amid the endless discussion of crime in the West we have to remind ourselves that the worst crimes in the twentieth century were either committed by governments or under government auspices. We now have an International War Crimes Tribunal, and even an International Criminal Court, though the United States refuses to sign up to this. Today former President Milošović appears before a human rights tribunal, but Pinochet has never done so, and wins support from prominent former cabinet ministers. Saddam Hussein is condemned, but no one has ever been tried for drenching the jungles of Vietnam and Cambodia with Agent Orange, or for training and equipping the murderous regimes of Central and South America in which hundreds of thousands of people died through torture or were executed in the most sadistic ways. The Libyan government has delivered those responsible for the Lockerbie bombing but the captain of the USS *Vincennes* who shot down the Iranian passenger jet which lay behind this atrocity has never faced charges. As we know, labels like 'war criminal' are applied to the losers in history. On the winning side crimes of obedience are called 'loyalty' though they may involve atrocious acts which on any objective standard ought to be prosecuted.

The comparison between the three forms of crime makes clear why some consider criminal justice to be merely the ideological reflection of the interests of powerful groups. The way in which street crime is the sole focus of government agencies suggests that the criminal justice system is actually a form of social control which makes sure that the powerless are more likely to be sent to prison and which creates the illusion that what the Victorians called 'the dangerous classes' are primarily located at the bottom of the social hierarchy. This is not to say that street crime is unimportant. Malcolm X described street criminals as 'Hyenas and wolves of the street'. They prey mainly on their fellow poor and they can make life intolerable in some environments. On the other hand, for the amount of social damage and misery caused, do they compare to the overall impact of the other forms of crime, or, for that matter, to the imposition of Structural Adjustment Programmes by the ideologies of the IMF?

Understanding crime

The priority of street crime on the political and criminological agenda means that the many attempts to understand crime tend to take street crime as normative. This, I have argued, is hardly the case. Many theories have been elaborated to seek to understand crime and I will outline them in what follows, without adopting any one of the many schemes on offer.

A theory with obvious prima facie plausibility traces a connection between street crime and poverty and poor social environments. The connection is obvious in the statistics. In Britain in 1991 83 per cent of prisoners were working class and 23 per cent had been in local authority care before the age of 16. In the United States a labourer is 14 times more likely to go to prison than the professional, the person with less than four years education 18 times more likely than the postgraduate. The unemployed are imprisoned disproportionately to the rest of the population. Most chronic offenders, it has been found, shared common childhood characteristics. They are more likely to have been rated as troublesome at school, to come from poor larger families and have experienced harsh or erratic parental discipline. Linked with all this it has been clear for well over a century that slums cause the social disorganization which gives rise to crime. By contrast, young people who are strongly attached to their school, who have high educational and occupational aspirations, or who are strongly attached to their parents are less likely to commit crime.

Drawing on such accounts, control theories of crime argue that human beings will seek the rewards of crime unless they are held in check or controlled. Crime is said to flow from low self-control and is found when the individual's bond to society is broken. By contrast, attachment, commitment, involvement and belief all function to socialize people and make crime less likely.

The problem with this type of theory is that it fails to account for the fact that the majority of the poor working class are not criminals, but struggle to live honestly, and the fact that, as we have seen, crime is not the prerogative of the working-class poor. It is also not the prerogative of the poorly socialized, in the sense that the powerful have every advantage, in that respect, that money can buy. The overwhelming honesty of the poor also tells against the Marxist argument that crime springs from the demoralization of the oppressed class. Likewise, research has established that middle-class offending goes well beyond trivial indiscretions. Child sex abuse, domestic violence, football hooliganism, workplace theft and drug offences are committed by people from all social classes. When we add the gender pattern to this (see below) it is clear that we cannot make a simple connection between poverty and crime. The rich ought to have a low crime rate but, arguably, do not, while poor women ought to be highly criminalized, but are not. On the other hand environment and social conditioning surely plays its part. Take the most obnoxious prisoner you can think of, and ask yourself what she or he would be like if they had been swapped in the cradle with Anne or Charles Windsor, and what would have happened if Anne or Charles Windsor had been put in their place. The reflection, I think, is instructive.

As noted, gender further complicates the argument from poverty and poor socialization. In a population of ten thousand people, it has been pointed out, the most accurate predictor of who will commit crime is gender. In 1999 in Britain 83 per cent of convictions were of men. It is the young adult male aged about twenty who is most likely to commit a crime of violence; a boy of fourteen who is most likely to be charged with theft. Only one in six young offenders is a woman. Reasons for this include the greater strength of men, greater opportunity because of the division of domestic labour, and gendered socialization, which makes some forms of crime an attractive 'dare' to young men. The 16-year-old shot dead by a farmer in Britain was on his first 'job' and had boasted to friends about it. He looked on it as a lark.

If we accept that nurture comes before nature, and that socialization has something to do with crime, then we would expect the rise of equality feminism to make some difference to these statistics. A 1994 report on female violence quoted a woman who had been jailed for grievous bodily harm, seriously wounding another girl with a knife, saying: 'For years men have had it all their own way, but now women are coming alongside, and I say, "good on them".' In relation to such attitudes one can only agree with those feminists who argue that a woman who aspires to be equal to men in this way lacks ambition. Fortunately, the statistical evidence for a rise in crimes of violence by women is slight. The impact of conventional socialization can be seen in the fact that the rate of offending for young women peaks earlier and recedes earlier than that of young men. Between 14 and 17 years of age the male–female ratio is 4:1, but by 22–25 it is 11:1. Courtship, marriage and motherhood doubtless account for this.

A more nuanced account of the relation between poverty and crime, currently widely accepted, emphasizes the connection between crime and relative deprivation. The old moralizing version of this, popular with evangelicals like Hannah More, traced crime to envy. More urged the poor to accept their lot and be grateful for what they had. On this account the decline of religion is a key part of the increase of crime. The ideological function of this 'explanation' scarcely needs comment.

Today it is emphasized that street crime occurs in a social climate dominated by free-market principles and the idea of 'rationally maximizing behaviour' creates an environment in which both street crime and suite crime flourish. A BBC report on Asian crime in Britain in January 2003, for example, interviewed a man depicted as one of the biggest drug suppliers in Britain. He saw his business, in which profits were laundered into respectable operations, as a perfectly reasonable way of making a living. If humans are motivated primarily by self-interest then crime is perfectly rational, a point of view which was already being argued by some sociologists at the beginning of the twentieth century. Crime, some have argued, arises principally from self-interest. All that is wrong with criminal behaviour is that it opts out of the social contract, and if everyone did that there would be no society. So-called opportunity theory makes the point that when society depicts material gain as the chief indicator of personal success then people will adopt illegitimate means to succeed if legitimate means, denied them by class or racial background, fail. Likewise assuming that people will always act dishonestly if given a chance, situational crime theory argues that crime depends on the availability of stealable goods. To prevent crime you basically need better security.

These accounts of crime are sympathetic to the view that capitalism is intrinsically criminogenic because its central goal is profit, because it makes material success the prime marker of the human good and because it encourages executives to subordinate their personal ethical codes to the imperatives of the organization. It was calculated in 1999 that 60 per cent of deaths from industrial injury in Britain were due to the pressures of the profit system (Slapper, 1999). Journalists in Britain found that three out of four high-street banks they approached were perfectly prepared to set up accounts with white supremacist groups, chemical weapons firms and child pornography (*Guardian*, 12 May 1995). Further, monopolies, or near monopolies, allow big firms to put retailers under huge pressure to make a living, causing smaller-scale fraud further down the line. Box (1983) agrees with the popular view that all power corrupts and that power itself is criminogenic. It corrupts our relationship to others, it makes the commission of crime easier, and it enlarges the scope of crime. In this respect the growth of corporation power is especially alarming. Against such contentions it is argued that it makes it difficult to explain the relative stability of economic trade within and between nations, but a number of noted defenders of the free market, such as George Soros and Joe Stiglitz, have recently argued that current developments in capitalism could lead to social chaos which would make all forms of legitimate trade impossible.

Jock Young argues that polarization in inequality is far more criminogenic than absolute deprivation, where large groups all share poverty together, and accept it as inevitable. Societies where large groups are marginalized and effectively denied equal opportunity foster criminal subcultures. Once part of a subculture, peer pressure then coerces people to live up to the expectations of that group. Where Hannah More read envy as the result of original sin, always more obvious in the lower classes than the upper, today 'strain theory' points out that crime occurs where there is cultural inclusion and structural exclusion. In a society based on quests for success, independence and self-sufficiency those who fail on all counts turn to alcohol and drugs and are easily involved in crime. As Young argues this demonstrates not their marginalization from society but the extent to which they have internalized the so-called 'American dream'. The problem with this explanation is, as we have seen, that it cannot account for the fact that the working class are basically law-abiding.

Psychiatric disorder is another obvious factor in many crimes. Among the sentenced male population in Britain 37 per cent have a diagnosable mental disorder. Among the remand population this figure rises to 63 per cent with 5 per cent being psychotic. Twenty per cent of female prisoners had been in psychiatric hospital prior to incarceration. A 1997 survey of 3,000 prisoners in England and Wales found 7 per cent of sentenced men and 10 per cent on remand to have psychotic disorders. Proportionately three times as many male prisoners display high scores for neurotic symptoms as in the population generally. Between one-third and one-half of all prisoners have used heroin. Between two-fifths and one-half report having been drug dependent in the year prior to incarceration. The majority of murderers are found to suffer either from severe mental strain or diagnosable psychiatric disorder; a third commit suicide before arrest. This is a fact which was always taken into account, in that someone had to be 'fit to be hanged', but contemporary understandings of what constitutes mental disorder are far wider than anything available before the mid-twentieth century. It throws a vivid light on what constitutes responsibility. If, instead of saying we are universally sinful, we say that none of us are fully integrated human beings, that we all have our neuroses and 'hang-ups', this reflects back not just on our understanding of crime but of sin. The Mennonite theologian Howard Zehr speaks of brokenness as the central fact of both victims and offenders. Our approach to brokenness is going to be very different from our approach to sin and wickedness. The concept of guilt which guides the justice process is narrow and primarily 'objective'. Did the accused commit the act as prescribed by law; was the act contrary to law? Did they intend to do it? You are either guilty or not guilty. Sociological and psychological perspectives are different and necessarily more nuanced but so, too, would be a perspective which took the reality of original sin seriously.

The concern with what does or does not count as deviance in some respects continues this concern. In the 1970s, 'New Deviancy Theory' followed psychiatrists like R. D. Laing and argued that what counts as normal is largely arbitrary. What is called crime represents the decision by some to label others in that way. People become what they are called. Deviance follows from being labelled rather than the other way round. Deviancy can be viewed as a break from the moral bind involved in ongoing normalized repression. The task is to create a society in which the facts of human diversity are not subject to the power to criminalize. But, as Malcolm X insisted, there are forms of anti-social behaviour which are properly rejected both by and on behalf of the poor.

Finally there are genetic or biological arguments of which the classic exponent was Lombroso, who argued that some people are born criminals, atavisms, throwbacks to a more primitive stage of society. 'The criminal' was a fact of nature who should be dealt with 'scientifically' perhaps by eugenics, so that criminality could eventually be eliminated. Ludicrous as Lombroso's theories were, today it is conceded that the idea that genetic make-up might dispose to criminality may not be entirely false. There is strong evidence, for example, based on unseparated twins, that criminality may be determined in this way. Were this to be the case it would be hard to avoid the conclusion that some people were 'born evil' in a way that others were not, and what becomes of responsibility then?

Crime, sin and responsibility

We have seen what part, at least, of the Christian tradition has meant by sin, and we have seen what criminologists consider to be crime and some of the ways they try to understand this. What is the connection? Given the dialectic of bondage and freedom might we, for example, say that *tout comprendre c'est tout pardonner*? If we understand the reasons for crime does it cease to be culpable? Does understanding dissolve the sense of sin? One of the factors which has most problematized Christian understandings of sin is the growing understanding, since Freud, of neurosis. Those who are whole have no need of a physician, but which of us is whole? Beyond reactionary populism current penal rhetoric stems in part from the account of the rational responsible agent, or of the guilty sinner, at the heart of traditional political theory and jurisprudence. What determines a guilty verdict, says the Western tradition of jurisprudence, is *mens rea*, evil intent. Despite the growth of social science and the ensuing vigorous debate about the significance of social determination over the past one hundred and fifty years an abstract view of human nature still informs key discussions of justice like that of John Rawls, still informs the ideology of criminal justice, with its key aim to weigh evidence and establish guilt or innocence, and still informs the discussion of criminal justice in Parliament and in the press. But what is the reality? Communities have arisen piecemeal, hand to mouth, responding to invasion and immigration, to changes in trade and technology, the strong and the wealthy calling the tune, writing existing power structures into their laws which then have to be chipped away at flake by flake. These are the communities which train us in the virtues, and to that extent, we might say, what chance do we have? Control theory, like some Christian groups, argues that the nurturance of loving, stable families is the key factor in avoiding crime. But how many human beings are born into those loving families with adequate material and educational resources to produce the paradigm 'rational, responsible agent'? To take a recent example, is someone whose parents split up when he was born, who is raised thinking his mother is his sister, who has not spoken to the grandfather who has brought him up for four years, unemployed, a repressed homosexual with no outlet for his emotions, likely to be a 'rational, responsible agent'? The name of this person was Thomas Hamilton, the killer of the schoolchildren at Dunblane. Those in society who tried to help him and integrate him into the community were attacked, after the event, for encouraging a fiend.

On the other hand, as I have argued, we cannot surrender responsibility. In a famous article C. S. Lewis argued that if crime is simply pathological it removes the concept of desert from punishment. Only as deserved or undeserved can a sentence be just or unjust. If crime is a disease which needs cure rather than sin which needs pardoning, mercy is eliminated. So responsibility is demanded if justice and mercy, the heart of Micah's account of shalom, is to be preserved. Again, an insistence on responsibility was at the heart of the Nuremberg trials, which refused to allow that obeying orders amounted to the kind of compulsion which constituted a defence of wicked acts. It is this insistence which forms the presupposition of the procedures of the new war crimes tribunal or the International Court of Human Rights. Calling to account in this way is an exact contemporary correlate of Amos' charge against the nations and in particular against the rich and powerful. Even here, however, what allowance are we to make for people in the grip of powerful ideologies, which we can understand as a form of the principalities and powers?

We come back to two points. We come back to original sin, our mutual involvement in systems which dehumanize us, which we do not choose or opt into, and which are simply part of the human condition. Following Augustine we will expect that to produce crime in any society, understanding crime here as a form of sin, as behaviour which mutilates or destroys the image of God in us. But we also come back to the Church, to the question of the person in community, and the fashioning of the kind of community which makes fully human behaviour possible. Here we return to that alternative tradition which thinks of the Church as exemplary community, as the community in which human beings are enabled to find true freedom and understand the nature of their bondage. Crime, we have seen, occurs throughout the structure of society, including the leadership, and its origins are to be found in that structure and its core values. 'Tackling crime' is part of the much larger agenda of creating a just society, a society in which the inequalities of wealth and power are done away with, the creation of shalom. The theological context for understanding crime, in other words, is only partially the doctrine of sin. More fundamentally it is what we mean by the kingdom of God.

5 | **Paying the Price**

A young man goes to a pub for a drink with his girlfriend. As he comes out a middle-aged man smashes his head with a claw hammer. After a month in intensive care he begins to make a recovery, but will never walk properly or work again. When the case comes to court it turns out the attacker was seeking revenge for someone who pushed a broken glass into his son's face. But he mistook his victim who had nothing whatever to do with this attack. The judge sentences him to eight years.

Or another case: two couples in their late twenties and early thirties befriend a gullible 14-year-old girl and use her as a sex slave. They begin to torture her with burns and needles, to starve her and force her to eat excrement. After some days they take her to a field, pour petrol over her and set her alight. Before she dies she is able to name her attackers. The judge sentences all four to fourteen years, 'life' in Britain.

Such cases, as we saw in the last chapter, are not everyday forms of crime. I cite them in the first instance because both cases involved offenders of mature age, who, as the judge in the first case remarked, ought certainly to have known better, and in both cases psychiatric reports discounted any question of obvious mental illness. In the second place, such crimes raise passionate feelings and the call for punishment and it is especially in relation to such crimes that judges are condemned for being too lenient. But consider this splendidly provocative polemic from the Dutch criminologist Herman Bianchi:

> The ideas of punishment and punitive response to liability acts must wither away entirely. The very thought that one grown up human being should ever have a right, or a duty, to punish another grown up human being is a gross indecency, and the phenomenon cannot stand up to any ethical test. (Bianchi, 1994, p. 341)

Is it really the case that punishment of such offenders is a gross inde-
cency? How should we respond to such crimes?

Perhaps the oldest answer, already part of the first story, is to take
vengeance. The instinct of vengeance is to hurt savagely. 'The firing
squad is too good for them,' said one newspaper headline after the
Omagh bombing. Vengeance has been robustly defended by a
humanist like John Carey as a proper societal response to wrong,
and it has also been argued that unless properly punitive responses
are made people will take justice into their own hands. But where
does vengeance stop? Perhaps with a view to preventing endless
feuding, the Hebrew Bible insisted that vengeance belonged to God
(Dt 32.35). On the other hand God is often spoken of as 'a God of
vengeance' who exercises vengeance on Israel and on wrongdoers in
general. The number of offences which were capital, which included
blasphemy, false prophecy, murder, assault on one's parents, rape,
adultery, sodomy and homosexuality, suggests that leaving
vengeance to God hardly proscribed savage punishment. On the
contrary, a vengeful God seems to beget vengeful punishments. The
lex talionis, an eye for an eye, was probably an attempt to limit the
scope of these and works on the principle of making the punishment fit the crime. To what extent it was intended literally, rather
than metaphorically, it is difficult to know.

The *lex talionis* involves suffering on the part of the offender.
Some philosophers argue that pain is definitional to punishment, as
opposed to being a by-product of vengeance or accident or misfortune. Punishment, they argue, must involve the deliberate infliction
of pain, or at least inconvenience, on the convicted person; it must
represent a response to an offence that was freely and knowingly
committed; it must be of an offender (the point being that in cases
of mistaken identity what happens is not punishment but injustice);
and it must be imposed by a legitimate authority (as opposed, say,
to the local vigilante group or, in Belfast, to paramilitary groups
enforcing their own codes). The pain involved in punishment, it is
argued, is an essential part of it, and not an accidental outcome.

Making pain definitional of punishment is contentious. On the
one hand many punishments are available to the courts which do
not involve pain in the obvious sense, which include care orders,
attendance centre orders, community service orders; and fines,
which are the most common form of punishment. 'Condemnation'
might be a better term than pain as it is the element of condemna-

tion which distinguishes between a tax and a fine. Others argue that hard treatment, pain in the proper sense, is essential if condemnation or censure is to be adequately conveyed. This certainly seems to be the majority view in contemporary Britain and North America where we live in highly punitive societies. At the end of the nineteenth century Durkheim was able to suggest that savage punishments were the preserve of 'less-developed' societies, while in more-developed societies punishment was tempered by mercy. One wonders what he would have made of the reintroduction of the chain gang in Arizona, or the 'three strikes and you're out' policy adopted in California. Durkheim seems to have thought of prison as a form of mercy and we can then ask whether he really understood what is involved in imprisonment. Criminologists from quite different positions, for example, have argued that once we recognize how severe any prison sentence is, a three-year term is a very harsh punishment whatever the conditions under which it is served. We should also note that while shame punishments were phased out in the early nineteenth century they have effectively been reintroduced through trial by tabloid journalism. Much sensational reporting, especially in sex-related cases, is a modern and far worse version of the Skimmington ride of which Thomas Hardy wrote.

In punitive societies such as ours punishment needs no justification. On the contrary, the tabloid press is ever watchful for any sign of leniency on the part of the judiciary and politicians, and such leniency is a certain vote loser. In Britain no Home Secretary was prepared to take the political risk of releasing the child murderer Myra Hindley though there were certainly no prudential reasons for keeping her in jail.

Punishment as the infliction of pain requires justification for a number of reasons. First, the infliction of pain is hardly a self-evident good. Rather, as Bentham put it, 'all punishment is mischief, all punishment in itself is evil'. Much of the clamour for punishment is an expression of the demand for vengeance, and vengeance is not moral even if it is ascribed to YHWH. Second, it is argued that punishment infringes on goods we take to be proper to our humanness such as autonomy, freedom and privacy. By failing to respect those values it could be argued that punishment calls them into question. Third, since street crime is the major focus of the courts, it is imposed differentially on the least powerful groups in society. Further, it is toughest where desert is least since amateurs and young people are the ones who get caught, while the serious professional criminals get away with it (some estimates of the successful solving of crime put this as low as 2 or 3 per cent). Finally, a point which we shall frequently come back to, many offenders have already suffered various kinds of material exclusion and their punishments often lead to further exclusion.

In relation to these points we need at once to object that the language of autonomy, commonplace in criminological discussion, cannot be accepted by the theologian. From the theological perspective people are not autonomous but, on the contrary, exist only as members one of the other. This applies when we think of our mutual involvement in original sin but also, conversely, in our learning of the virtues. The point which philosophers want to make about autonomy is better made, theologically, by insisting that the Church is always primarily interested in human beings rather than causes and that since 'man' is the measure of all things because the Son of man became human, even the most wretched person must be resolutely defended against the autocracy of every cause or bureaucracy.

Why, then, should offenders be punished? A whole variety of reasons are adduced. Because society cannot turn a blind eye to the assumption that 'crime pays'; because offenders deserve it; because we have to stop people committing further crimes; because crime should be denounced; because we have to reassure the victim that society cares about what has happened; because we have to protect society from dangerous or dishonest people; because we have to allow offenders to make amends for the harm they have caused; to ensure that the laws are obeyed; because criminals have to repay their debt to society; because balance may be restored; so that expiation, atonement or annulment of crime may be made.

In these various justifications there is a tension between reasons based on preventing crime and those which assume that offenders must be punished because they deserve it. These are the so-called consequentialist and retributive justifications of punishment. The idea of punishment as a kind of 'communication' has also recently made a strong showing. I shall not follow these strictly, but add some headings, which seems to me of more interest to the theological discussion.

Reasons for punishment

i. Denunciation

In the second chapter we encountered Durkheim's view of law as an expression of social solidarity. It followed from that that a crime was any act which offended against social solidarity and punishment, in turn, was the reflex in which society turned passionately against the offender. The emotions of anger or indignation should not be regarded as irrational but recognized as proper responses to some states. As an account of why people feel punitive this is helpful though it does not address the question of whether such reactions are justified. On Durkheim's account the social is the true sacred, and so serious crimes are a breach of sacred values, but the obverse of the sacred is the idolatrous. Perhaps the passionate condemnation of offences ends up sacrificing people to a fetish. Here the case for the cool objectivity of law and the legal process is strong.

Lord Denning essentially agreed with this view, speaking of punishment as the way in which society expresses its denunciation of wrongdoing. Judges, obviously, are the spokespersons of this denunciation. Denning argued that the scale of punishment ought to be graded according to the revulsion felt by the great majority of citizens to the crimes committed. In a slightly different point he argued that unless this happened respect for law would not be maintained. But how do you judge the scale of revulsion in an age dominated by the tabloid press and the mass media? Their claim to be the *vox populi* is problematized by facts of ownership as well as by their obvious contempt for ethical standards in other areas, from sex ethics to privacy laws. And can judges, who almost without exception come from social classes one and two, speak for society in this way? The gospel prohibition of judgement warns us about the moral dangers involved in the process. Pronouncing judgement may be socially necessary but it is certainly morally perilous, constituting as it does an invitation to forget that we are made of the same clay as the offender. This moral peril is reinforced when judgement is attended, as it is in Britain, by all the trappings of power. To put it sharply, is it possible to be a judge and not be morally corrupted?

A similar justification of punishment, which focuses on our membership of a community rather than on denunciation, argues that the offender must suffer because wrongdoing alters our relations to them, and behaving as if nothing had happened denies the

real implications of their actions. This is a crucial point for abolition-
ists like Bianchi to address. Some argue that in contemporary society
justice amounts to respecting difference. The question here is that if
difference is too great the norms which make society workable at all
simply are not in place. Beyond difference there has to be some
agreement on common values for society to survive. Wrongdoing, it
is argued, breaches this agreement. Society is a complex web of
relations and it depends for its very existence on those relations
being honoured. If we flout those relations, and the values they
embody, then we exclude ourselves from community and call the
viability of society into question. Punishment, on this account, is a
reaffirmation of the core values that keep society in being.

An obvious objection to such accounts is to point to the fractured
nature of any known society. Durkheim, Denning and others who
argue in this way seem to presuppose a view of society as a har-
monious whole, but society is not like that. It is formed by a network
of competing and conflicting subcultures and classes. If we think of
the eighteenth-century poaching laws, for example, who is the 'we'
who was outraged by the offence? What is being denounced? The
example raises in an extreme way the question of what class interests
are being defended by the law, and I shall have to return to this
question again. We can also ask why *punishment* is necessary to
denounce crime. Might other practices do that? If denunciation and
the reaffirmation of community values is what is at stake one could
imagine forms of communication which did the same job, and indeed
the Book of Common Prayer seems to have thought of the homily as
functioning in something like this way. Of course, there is the
question whether that is adequate, but at the very least we have to say
that punishment is not the self-evident means of attaining this goal.

ii. Deterrence

So-called consequentialist accounts of punishment concentrate on
deterrence or incapacitation. The consequentialist approach to
ethics, which originated in the eighteenth century as a means of
getting away from what were assumed to be the irrational dictates of
religious commands, judges the morality or otherwise of an act by
its effect on the body politic, or in Bentham's classic formulation, by
whether it promotes the greatest happiness of the greatest number.
In Britain the Royal Commission on capital punishment in 1953
defended the death penalty on the grounds both that it deterred

individuals tempted to commit murder, but also that it built up in the community, over a long period of time, a deep feeling of peculiar abhorrence for the crime of murder. As Fitzjames Stephen put it in the nineteenth century, 'That men are hung for murder is one great reason why murder is considered so dreadful a crime.'

There are two problems with the argument, practical and moral. The practical problem is that the empirical evidence is that harsh punishments do not deter crime. Rather the opposite, the more severe the punishment the greater the lengths to which the offender is tempted to go in order to escape it. In fact such evidence as we have indicates that the probability of detection is more significant than the severity of punishment. What deters crime is not punishment but fear of detection. So Lord Windlesham, a former chair of the Parole Board, said in 1996:

> In over six years on the Parole Board I saw case after case, including many of the most serious offences of violence, which had been committed on impulse or under the influence of drugs or alcohol. There had been no prior thought whatever of the consequences if the crime were to be detected . . . Even when crimes are planned in advance by identifiable professional criminals, often known to the police, it is the risk of detection and conviction that counts for more in any calculation of the risks and benefits than the likely penalty.

More than a century earlier Marx had remarked ironically that since Cain the world has been neither intimidated nor ameliorated by punishment.

At least since Kant people have expressed unease about the morality of deterrence. The root of the word 'deterrence' is terror and implies frightening people into good behaviour. As we saw when thinking about law, this is not a moral way of proceeding. It thinks of law in terms of threats and therefore assumes that people have to be dealt with in that way. 'To base justification of punishment on threats', said Hegel, 'is to liken it to the act of a man who lifts a stick against a dog. It is to treat a man like a dog instead of with the freedom and respect due to a man.' It fails to treat the citizen as a rational and autonomous agent.

Incapacitation has similar kinds of problems. It seems that, first, we are wrong about twice as often as we are right in predicting re-offending. Second, the evidence is that we can never catch enough criminals to reduce crime substantially through incapacitation. It too has profound moral problems. Defenders of the idea point to the idea of quarantine, which, they argue, is analogous to incapacitation, but it is extremely questionable to punish someone for something they might commit rather than something they have in fact committed. In a notorious case in the eighteenth century a judge told a condemned man that he was not being hanged for stealing a sheep but that sheep might not be stolen. The immorality of such punishment is at the heart of the retributivist insistence that only offenders should be punished and only when guilt is established. There is a clear need for some types of dangerous offender to be detained but the number of these is probably quite small.

Interestingly it has been argued that, for all its flaws, deterrence is effective as a response to corporate crime. This kind of crime is not usually one-off but chronic, involving such things as the falsification of records or the failure to maintain proper safety standards. In such cases the message of deterrence is received by those who need to hear it, which is not the case in street crime, and sentencing, when it happens, does not exacerbate social inequality. Slapper and Tombs (1999) therefore call for greater regulation and enforcement in the area of corporate crime.

iii. Punishment as a moral need

An approach to punishment which goes right back to Plato's understanding of the perils of injustice is that punishment is a moral need. Both Hegel and Kierkegaard shared this view but it receives its strongest expression, in the twentieth century at any rate, from Simone Weil in the book she wrote for de Gaulle and the Free French, *The Need for Roots*. Beginning with community she argued that crime places us outside the chain of obligations which bind every human being to every other one. Punishment, in her view, is what welds the offender back into the community. To punish someone is to respect them, by showing that we still consider them part of the community. Punishment, in her view, ought to be an honour. It both wipes out the stigma of crime, and must be regarded as a supplementary form of education, compelling a higher devotion to the public good.

Punishment, then, takes the wrongdoer seriously as a moral agent, and a sane offender has a right to be punished rather than manipulated or ignored. Punishment seeks to prevent continuation in hardness of heart, and to promote a return to goodness. It is a 'transforming agent'. In a similar vein others have spoken of punishment as a symbol, an outward and visible sign of an inward and spiritual disgrace, which seeks both to forestall the consummation of wrongdoing and to promote its annulment.

Weil herself went on to set out the objections to this kind of argument citing the discredit attaching to the police, the irresponsible conduct of the judiciary, the prison system, the permanent social stigma cast upon ex-convicts, the scale of penalties which provides a much harsher punishment for ten acts of petty larceny than for one rape or certain types of murder, and which even provides punishments for ordinary misfortune. All this, she argued, made punishment of this ideal type impossible. In an unjust society the relative degree of immunity should increase, not as you go up, but as you go down the social scale because otherwise the hardships inflicted will be felt to be in the nature of constraints or even abuses of power, and will no longer constitute punishments. For there to be punishment there has to be justice. What she was calling for, therefore, was a complete reordering of society.

iv. Retribution

The last thirty years of the twentieth century marked a large-scale return to retributivism, the basic insight of which is that criminals must get their just deserts. This theory can find strong theological expression arguing that crime is an offence against God and the ultimate function of punishment is to acknowledge God's Lordship and vindicate God's honour. Those who argue in this way appear to believe that dehumanizing treatment of offenders remains somehow compatible with God's honour.

The idea of just deserts is a very ancient insight, as the *lex talionis* shows, but it is not a very clear one for all that. What is it about sin or crime which calls for such payment? It has been suggested that crime represents taking an unfair advantage of the rest of society, but this is a very odd description of many types of crime (for example rape). On some readings Kant believed that society was based on a social contract from which all benefited and that crime is an activity which improperly breaches that contract. Punishment then restores the proper balance between benefit and obedience to the laws by which we all live. I shall take up the metaphor of balance later but, again, it is not self-evidently true. It seems to rest on the idea that a certain amount of suffering atones for suffering inflicted, the *lex talionis* again, so that the scales between two parties are made level once more. The survival of the *lex talionis* over three millennia shows that it is not simple nonsense but it does seem to be a way of saying, as George Bernard Shaw put it, that two blacks make a white. 'We get the grotesque spectacle', he wrote, 'of a judge committing thousands of horrendous crimes in order that thousands of criminals may feel that they have balanced their moral accounts.' A more promising account of why punishment is intrinsically called for by wrongdoing is that it introduces a sense of closure to events in which harm has been done. In so doing it enables life to go on as before. Again, however, one would have to ask whether there were other ways for that to happen.

The return to retributivism was premised partly on the failure of utilitarian and preventionist criminology to deliver on its promises and reduce crime and partly on a reaction to the penal practice of the 1960s which assumed that offenders were social or moral deviants who needed to be treated or normalized. In a famous manifesto published in 1971, *Struggle for Justice*, the North American Quakers asked for justice rather than treatment. They wanted determinate sentences for specific offences rather than treatments in which the therapist would not release you until you were well. In their wake some theologians have also objected to the rhetoric of therapy replacing that of guilt and forgiveness. In view of its commitment to justice, it is argued, Christianity has a stake in retribution.

The moral case against retributivism is, however, strong. In the first place, the infliction of pain is agreed to be an evil. Is it really the case that there is intrinsic good in the guilty suffering? Is retribution state-authorized retaliation? Second, retributivists argue that offenders forfeit their claim to freedom from suffering but, it has been pointed out, a judge who violates someone's right to a fair trial does not thereby forfeit their own right to a fair trial (Braithwaite and Pettit, 1990). Violation of the rights of others is not equivalent to justifying one's own loss of rights. Third, although retributivists speak of just deserts, there is no agreed scale which assigns so much punishment for such and such an act. As the Norwegian criminologist Thomas Mathiesen asks ironically, how many years of a person's liberty equals the value of a lost television set? The vagueness of the rhetoric of desert masks mistakes which have a huge impact on people's lives.

v. Reform

In Britain some seventy years of the hard-bed and hard-board philosophy was brought to a close by the Gladstone Committee in 1895 and the Criminal Justice Bill which followed that. The Committee argued that prison treatment should be effectually designed 'to maintain, stimulate, or awaken the higher susceptibilities of prisoners and turn them out of prison better men and women, both physically and morally, than when they came in'. Writing five years later the theologian R. C. Moberly argued that unless punishment had in view the rehabilitation of the offender it was immoral. Without that aim, he said, it was equivalent to vengeance, and vengeance was always wrong. On both sides of the Atlantic such arguments ushered in the penal welfare era.

Belief in reformation was, of course, deeply rooted in some Christian approaches to offenders, which regarded them as sinners who needed to be saved. Arguments for solitude, for regular homilies, for useful work, were all part of this process. That labour was in some way redemptive was an idea that went back to the bridewells and houses of correction and beyond that to the Hebrew Bible. Later came the enthusiasm for physical education as something which promoted moral reform, and later still came counselling and psychotherapy.

The emphasis on reform was never unchallenged. Worries about brainwashing, familiar from the communist bloc, were extended to the jail. Anthony Burgess, in *A Clockwork Orange*, depicted a nightmare scenario where men in white coats tried to normalize violent offenders, a process which happened, he implied, at the end of the novel, simply by mainstream processes of socialization, by marriage and 'settling down'. As we have seen, C. S. Lewis argued that to be cured against one's will is to be put on the level of those who have not attained the age of reason. Reform, it was argued, was an interference with the privacy and liberty of the individual. Lewis's view was ambiguous, one critic wryly noted, as to whether he would allow a convicted murderer his own choice between the indignity of reformation or the dignity of hanging.

A different but even more damaging objection to the idea of rehabilitation was that it simply did not work. Martinson's famous

1974 study concluded that the huge range of rehabilitative programmes on offer at the time had scarcely any impact on recidivism.
He himself later qualified this scepticism and the doctrine should
not proceed from 'nothing works' to 'do nothing'. Cohen's semi-
humorous summary of the position is that most things don't work
very well; some things work moderately; we're not sure what works
better than anything else; doing less is probably better than doing
more. But as he goes on to argue, much of what is provided by way
of rehabilitation is simply what the middle class take for granted
and some things, like literacy education or the provision of skills, is
surely uncontentious (Cohen, 1985, pp. 179, 259).

More recently this objection has been countered with the view
that rehabilitation is not something which is imposed on someone
but something which is offered them. The offender's moral freedom
is respected in their freedom to turn down the offer. Moreover, as in
the original impulse to rehabilitation, awareness of the offender's
background is involved, rather than the abstract question of
whether or not the offence was just a matter of free will. In this way,
social justice is integrated into criminal justice. From a quite different standpoint rehabilitation has been criticized as being too soft on
offenders; imposing treatment which may not reflect the seriousness
of the offence and as tending to blame society rather than holding
offenders accountable.

vi. Communication

R. A. Duff argues that we should come at the question of punishment by asking what it is to blame someone. The purpose of blame
is to persuade a person by the process of moral argument, hoping to
get them to accept the moral reasons by which they are judged and
to amend their behaviour accordingly. The person who accepts
blame feels the pain of guilt which follows from their new understanding of their conduct. Punishment, Duff argues, works in the
same way. It addresses the criminal as a rational moral agent, seeks
their understanding and assent and aims at repentance and reformation by communicating the reasons which justify it (Duff, 1986).

On Duff's account punishment is communicative, retributive and
reformative. It is *communicative* in that it seeks to communicate to
the criminal a proper understanding of their crime, helping them
to see the harm they have done to others and to themselves. It is
retributive in that it conveys a judgement on their crime. It is

reformative in that it aims to bring the offender to repent their crime, to accept their punishment and thus to reform. Punishment, then, should be understood as a species of secular penance that aims not just to communicate censure but thereby to persuade offenders to repentance, self-reform and reconciliation. It is, to anticipate a theme of the next chapter, inclusionary rather than exclusionary.

It can be objected to this account that it seems to presuppose the rational responsible agent of classical retributive theory. How is it to cope with the devious, the sullen, the defiant, the offender who rationalizes their offence away by arguing that the victim 'had it coming' or that their property was insured and so forth? Surely this profile is more true of most offenders than the one Duff presupposes? If the offender is repentant, on the other hand, what need is there of punishment? Simone Weil would respond, of course, that they would embrace it as an honour. It could also be objected that the target most law-makers seem to want to communicate with is the voter and the tabloid press, and what they want to communicate is that 'something is being done'. Against this imperative the moral demands of the system of punishment fade into insignificance. This is the negative side of the strong prioritization of community in this account of punishment, something which can be overlooked in some forms of retributivism where the emphasis is just on the offender and the need for him or her to be punished. It also thinks of law not primarily as command but as an appeal to our moral selves, as educative. In terms of the twofold account of what it means to be human with which I began, it clearly opts for the second model.

Atonement as a way of dealing with offending

One very prominent reading of the Christian Scriptures is that they are centrally concerned with dealing with offending. We saw that there were many capital offences in ancient Israel, some of which took the form of stoning, the point of which was the involvement of the whole community in the punishment. A response on the part of the offender, on the other hand, was to seek to make atonement. Sins committed with a high hand, in other words, sins where the issue of *mens rea* was indisputable, could not be atoned for, but sins committed in ignorance could be. Repentance atoned for sins of omission; repentance and sacrifice atoned for the transgression of a prohibition; repentance, sacrifice and suffering atoned for a trans-gression which merits destruction at God's hand; and repentance, sacrifice, suffering and death are together necessary for atonement when a person has profaned the name of God. A criminal atoned for his sins if, before his execution, he declared, 'May my death be an atonement [*kappara*] for all my sins.' The word used for atonement here is related to the word Paul uses to speak of the death of Christ. Let us remind ourselves of the famous verses in Romans:

> For there is no distinction, since all have sinned and fall short of the glory of God; they are now justified by his grace as a gift, through the redemption that is in Christ Jesus, whom God put forward as a sacrifice of atonement [*hilasterion*] by his blood, effective through faith. (Rom 3.23–5)

All the translations have difficulty with the word *hilasterion* but what is happening is clear enough. The old vocabulary of 'covering over' or wiping away sin, which applied in the first instance to ritual offences, is now applied to the death of Christ, understood as an expiation for sin. Christ's death has 'atoning power'. What sense can we make of this? If we take the most serious and sadistic murders, let us say those committed by Brady and Hindley, what would atone for that offence or 'cover it over'? Could the death of Christ be said to atone for it? If not, is it irredeemable? We have the famous protest of Ivan in *The Brothers Karamazov* where Dostoevsky wants to say that there are some sins which are unforgivable. Might atonement be something which makes forgiveness possible where previously it was not possible? Might the death of Christ be thrown 'into the balance' to change the situation in regard to the possibility of for-giveness? But what would that mean? Traditionally Christianity has argued that Christ's death was vicarious, that it atoned for others. We have to note that that runs counter to most of the arguments about punishment which we have been considering which think in terms of autonomy. Indeed, it is generally assumed today that vicarious punishment is neither possible nor moral.

That Christ atones for my sin has never, of course, meant that repentance was unnecessary. Rather, 'Repent and believe in the gospel' has always remained the heart of the good news. Perhaps, then, we can understand the language of expiation in terms of, first, its demonstration of the divine love which, second, calls the offender into a different kind of community which operates by forgiveness rather than exclusion. Of course as an account of how the Church has actually behaved or constituted itself, right up to the present, that invites rather hollow laughter. Nevertheless, as John Milbank has argued (1990), the Church ought to provide an alternative social space where a different, forgiving and restitutionary practice is pursued. This is 'atoning' in the sense that it involves recognition that sin or crime is not an individual matter, but an affair of the whole community and needs the whole community to cancel it.

A second metaphor which lies at the heart of Scripture, and especially of Jesus' teaching, is debt. Jesus teaches his disciples: 'Forgive us our debts as we forgive those who are indebted to us.' This metaphor probably has its origins in the experience of debt slavery in ancient Israel, and the Jubilee legislation, whether or not it was ever implemented, was aimed at periodically re-creating a debt-free society. It is a short step from there to regarding all offences as forms of debt and thinking of ways in which they can be cancelled. The power of the idea is in the emphasis on mutual indebtedness, and therefore on the idea of a society where debt cancellation, which is to say forgiveness, becomes practical politics.

In the tradition of the Church, though not in Scripture, the metaphor of balance has played a large part:

> Upon the cross, those scales most true,
> He paid the price for sinners due.

The sin of the world has flung down one side of the scales of justice. Christ's death restores the balance. In the various accounts of punishment we have seen this notion of restoring the balance, which goes back to ancient notions of justice as equality of experience, repeatedly expressed. Anselm's famous account of the atonement, *Cur Deus Homo?*, argues that Christ's death makes satisfaction for human sin and thereby repairs a damaged beauty or wholeness in God's creation. The power of suffering and death is crucial to his argument, as well as the pre-emptive love of God. It answers to the need to say that we cannot simply forgive sin, that, to use Anselm's phrase, its seriousness has to be recognized. But perhaps, rather than the death of Christ paying for human sin, it is more the case that we learn something both about the nature of sin and how to deal with it creatively. That Christ can die saying 'Father forgive them' is the point rather than God the Father weighing the merits of Christ's death over against 'the sins of the whole world'.

The different practice the Church is called to embody includes a different response to offences, as indicated by Jesus' teaching on the need to love our enemies. This, Walter Wink has argued, can be understood in terms of the need to come to terms with our shadow. Our enemies hold up a mirror to the unacceptable part of ourselves.

> As we become aware of our projections on our enemies, we are freed from the fear that we will overreact murderously toward them. We are able to develop an objective rage at the injustices they are perpetrating while still seeing them as children of God. The energy squandered nursing hatred becomes available to God for confronting the wrong or transforming the relationship. (Wink, 1992, p. 273)

Beyond punishment?

Must we punish? The ultimate goal in dealing with offenders is to bring them to an understanding of the consequences of their acts, and to take responsibility for them. Beyond that, in ways which we will consider in Chapter 8, ways need to be found for them to make atonement. Does punishment help them to do that? There are two good reasons for thinking that it does not. First, it is often observed that punishment, far from bringing people to repentance, actually hardens them. 'Generally speaking,' said Nietzsche, 'punishment makes men hard and cold; it concentrates; it sharpens the feeling of alienation; it strengthens the power of resistance . . . punishment *tames* men, but it does not make them "better".' Shaw agreed, arguing that to punish someone retributively was to injure them, 'and men are not improved by injuries'. Punishment very often makes people think of themselves rather than their victims and equally often it hurts innocent members of the offender's family. Weil thinks of it as purifying, but it can embitter and break as well. The Norwegian criminologist Nils Christie speaks of Western law as 'pain law' because it is an elaborate mechanism for administering 'just' doses of pain. Why do we do that? Because we have been educated to believe that humiliation and suffering are what justice is about and that evil must be held in check by harshness rather than by love and understanding. This stands up to the scrutiny neither of experience nor of moral sense. If the offender needs to learn that they are a person who matters, who has both the capacity and the responsibility to make good choices, who ought to respect others and cope peacefully with frustration and conflict, they are unlikely to do that if they are dealt with by violence. Violence breeds nothing but violence. The need to explore alternatives is urgent, and I explore some of these in Chapter 8.

Second, as we have seen at a number of points, punishment is extremely questionable in an unjust society. Judges and magistrates mete out punishment in the name of a community which, in its complacent acceptance of racism, gross inequality and gross imbalance of power, is deeply implicated in the manufacture of criminality in the first place. Like Simone Weil Duff argues that punishment would not be justifiable until we have brought about deep social, political, legal and moral changes in ourselves and our society. To those who maintain that we can, without injustice, preserve enough of our existing system of law to avert disaster he replies that this shows an unwarranted optimism either about the extent to which existing legal institutions and practices can be adequately justified or about the likely consequences of abandoning them – namely, anarchy and social disintegration (Duff, 1986, p. 297). He opts for the Augustinian view that punishment is a tragic necessity and not something about which we can ever have an easy conscience. Criminal punishment requires both a serious collective commitment to reform the content and operation of the penal system and a serious collective commitment to remedy the kinds of exclusion that undermine the preconditions of criminal liability and punishment. Without that it cannot be justified.

Some have argued, not for increasing increments in criminal justice, but for decrements – less criminal law, less police surveillance, less prosecution, less punishment – until solid evidence emerges that crime increases as a result. Society should, it is argued, aim to enhance the autonomy and freedom of individuals as far as possible and therefore the state should be minimally interventionist until the evidence is clear that more intrusive practices are required to do that. The offender should be explicitly sentenced only to that deprivation of liberty needed to protect the freedom and autonomy of others. This argument appeals to both a principle of parsimony, so that the onus of proof is always on the side of justifying criminal justice intrusions not on the side of justifying their removal, and the need to check the power of prison administrators to argue that any additional deprivation of liberty is wrong. As we shall see in the next chapter, the argument also calls for the reintegration of offenders as the primary goal of the criminal justice system. On the other hand it is conceded that it would not be possible to persist indefinitely with decrements to the criminal justice system without reaching the point where adverse consequences for crime will become evident (Braithwaite and Pettit, 1990).

Let us return to the crimes with which I began this chapter. Ought they to be punished? While I agree both with the decremental thesis and with the need to search for alternatives it remains unclear, in relation to such crimes, that the abolitionist perspective is self-evidently correct. Perhaps Augustine was right and punishment remains, sometimes, a tragic necessity which society cannot avoid. The rationale for it will be neither retributivism nor punishment as moral need, both of which fail on account of the injustice of punishment in a class society. If we are going to justify it in relation to atrocious crimes it seems to me we have to appeal partly to denunciation, which amounts to an emphatic assertion of what the community believes to be truly human behaviour, and partly communication, aimed at bringing the offender to understand the ways in which their behaviour has compromised true humanness. As R. C. Moberly argued, any punishment which does not aim at reformation is vengeance, and this is immoral. The analogy to punishment as communication in the disciplinary practice of the early Church is instructive in this regard. Putting it in that way, of course, makes nonsense of most of the punishment that does in fact go on. This is particularly true in relation to our normal form of punishment, imprisonment, to which I now turn.

6 | **Prison**

Until the eighteenth century, prisons were, for the most part, lock-ups. People might languish in them for a very long time, as Paul may have done, but they were not themselves a form of punishment. People were whipped, branded, had limbs lopped off, fined, put in the stocks or the pillory, banished, transported, executed – but jail itself was not part of the punishment, not an independent sentence. The emergence of the prison as a form of punishment can be read in a number of different ways. It can be read, for example, as the abandonment of a savage and primitive system of death, mutilation and shame for a more rational and humane system primarily aimed at reform. It had both religious and secular inspirations. North American Quakers, for example, developed houses of correction in place of corporal punishment, while Beccaria represented the Enlightenment rejection of corporal punishment in favour of a rational calculation of the time which needed to be served.

It can also be read as the penal correlate of the factory system. Both prison and the factory require discipline and here and there prisons have been used for industrial production. There is a correspondence between receiving reward for labour by the hour and paying for crime by 'doing time'. There are also strong correlations between levels of unemployment and prison populations, between periods of economic depression and the harshness of prison life for men on the one hand and reduced imprisonment for women on the other (in order to keep families together).

In recent times the master narrative for the rise of the prison has been provided by Michel Foucault who read it in a more sinister way as a key part of the emergence of governmentality, a new kind of penal rationality. Jeremy Bentham sketched out what he called a 'panopticon', a radial building where one warder could look into the cells of all the prisoners, so supplementing regulation with self-regulation. This design, Foucault argues, gives us a clue to the direction in which the whole of society was moving. Society becomes a carceral archipelago where all members of the population are subject to a disciplinary regulation. Like Hamlet's Denmark, society is a prison, and the prison itself is a symbol of the whole. As an object of knowledge the prisoner, too, is a type of us all, increasingly subject to surveillance. A new discipline arises, criminology, designed to classify and find solutions for crime. Contrary to the claims of prison reformers the new form of penality does not punish less but better, with more universality and necessity, inserting the power to punish more deeply into the social body. Foucault's great inspiration was Nietzsche, but this vision sounds more like Kafka.

Since Foucault others have argued that the intentions of penal reformers, legislators and practitioners always result in more control, less freedom, more persons under surveillance for greater portions of their lives. Tagging and electronic monitoring turn homes into prisons rather than keeping people out of prison and at home. Social welfare is not the creation of a caring state but a euphemism for, and one of the most efficient modes of, social control.

Foucault wrote during a decade which saw a growth of community corrections and the supposition that prison would become a less central institution. Probation, intermediate treatment and community service would, it was hoped, increasingly take the place of imprisonment. This could be read benignly, but with Foucaultian spectacles it can also be regarded as the imposition of dispersed discipline aimed at normalization. What was happening, it is argued, was not so much decarceration but transcarceration, all of these alternative forms of dealing with offenders representing an extension of the state's power.

Economic recession and a lurch to the political right brought these trends to an end. Retributivism returned to the agenda. Now sociologists of crime talk of penal populism and governing through crime. People are routinely sceptical of governments – politicians come bottom in polls which ask who people respect in society. In this context politicians can play to the gallery, exploit the fear of crime and thus seek re-legitimation. The result has been the second great incarceration, which has provoked no public outcry, the return of hard labour, the reintroduction of shaming techniques such as the wearing of uniforms while on labour assignments in the community, and even the chain gang. What has been called a decivilizing trend is in evidence with strategies of punishment which exhibit vengeance and cruelty. The death penalty has become common, currently running at two executions per week in the United States. The crime control industry becomes a major business. In the United States as a whole imprisonment rates are five times higher than in 1972 and six to ten times higher than in most European countries. Currently, as we saw, there are now in excess of 2 million people behind bars. Unsurprisingly, those states spending least on welfare have the highest imprisonment rates. Britain, with more than 73,000 people currently in prison, relies on imprisonment to a greater extent than any other country in Western Europe. In 1999, 125 persons were incarcerated per 100,000 of the population compared to 95 in Germany, 89 in France, 75 in the Netherlands and 59 in Sweden.

Michael Howard, British Home Secretary in 1995, was a spokesman for this trend when he said:

> Let us be clear. Prison works. It ensures that we are protected from murderers, muggers and rapists – and it makes many who are tempted to commit crime think twice. Prisons are a reminder to all of what will befall them if they break the law.

Let us ask what kind of reminder they are. I look first at the prisoners, then at prisons, and their rationale, before reflecting on the prisoner as scapegoat.

The prisoners

One of the central conundrums of prisons in a class-divided society is that the bulk of prisoners come from social classes four and five. This means that prisons are a feature and hazard of working-class life. In Britain in 1999, 60 per cent of prisoners were below NVQ level one in literacy and 75 per cent below in numeracy. Just to be clear, this means that the majority had a reading age of about eleven. In the gospels this group appear as the *ochlos*, the crowd, those on whom Jesus had compassion because they lacked shepherds. A class-divided society is structured in such a way that people in this group commit the crimes which land them in jail. The anti-sentimentalists will object that among this group are to be found the vicious and the remorseless, those who continue to use power to abuse others in prison. True, but even more of the vicious and remorseless are outside prison; some of them are in power; and some of them, church history teaches us, are to be found in the Church.

Prisoners are overwhelmingly young (average age 28), male, socially and economically disadvantaged, repetitive property offenders. In Britain men constitute 92 per cent of all receptions and 94 per cent of average daily population (ADP). At the same time, in the current great incarceration, women's imprisonment rates are rising. The largest increase is for sentences under six months, given for non-violent property offences, offences which a decade ago would have attracted probation orders. At the end of 2001 there were over 4,000 women in prison, a 150 per cent increase over 10 years compared with a 40 per cent increase for men.

In Britain 19 per cent of male prisoners and 25 per cent of female prisoners are members of ethnic minorities, two-thirds Afro-Caribbean. Black residents are imprisoned at roughly eight times the rate of white residents. Within all the ethnic minority groups the proportion of drug offenders is significantly higher than that of whites. In 1993 in Britain a black offender was 17 times as likely to get a custodial sentence as a white one. In the United States as a whole, at present, one in three black males in their twenties are either in prison, on parole or on probation in any given 12-month period.

The sort of crime that leads to imprisonment is largely the activity of adolescents and young adults, and sentences of imprisonment are generally imposed on repeat offenders: two-thirds of the offenders sentenced to immediate custody have three or more previous convictions, over a quarter have eleven or more.

Women tend to be imprisoned for trivial offences more often than men. A much publicized study in 1997 instanced the case of a 33-year-old mother of five, unable to work because of severe kidney and liver illness, sentenced to 14 days imprisonment for failing to pay a £190 fine for using 'apparatus for wireless telegraphy' (i.e. TV) without a licence. After sentence she was unable to contact her family and taken straight to prison in a state of extreme distress from where she was released after five days. Actions under the Wireless Telegraphy Act constitute 69 per cent of all summary prosecutions for women and only 17 per cent for men. The authors of the study made the point that the evidence is that all sections of society try to get away with not paying the licence fee, but that those who appear in court are disproportionately poor, unemployed, single parents and females. They comment that in this way criminal law serves symbolically to control part of the underclass while serving neither the recovery of lost revenue nor the creation of more responsible citizens.

In 1994 almost half the average daily population were serving 4 years or more and those serving 10 years or more numbered 7,000. In 1965 when the death penalty was abolished 88 prisoners got more than 10 years; in 2000 there were 262 such prisoners.

All forms of prisoners form a highly vulnerable group. As we saw in Chapter 4, there is a question of whether what we see is a crime event or a social need event. A study on psychiatric morbidity in prisoners in 1997 found that 48 per cent of the sentenced female population had experienced violence at home, 31 per cent had experienced sexual abuse, 40 per cent had received help for mental, nervous or emotional problems in the year before they came to prison, and 20 per cent of women on remand had been in psychiatric hospital at some time in their lives. Sir David Ramsbotham's review of women's imprisonment in the same year found that 70 per cent had no employment before coming to jail and 40 per cent had harmed themselves intentionally or attempted suicide; 75 per cent were serious drug misusers. The overall picture of the prison population, therefore, is one of multiple deprivation, social stress and either neurosis or psychosis. As a group prisoners are seriously disadvantaged before their imprisonment and their social marginality is heightened by their incarceration.

The same report found that 66 per cent of women in prison were mothers with children under 16, the care of whom was often unsettled. Unlike male prisoners most women prisoners are primary carers. Roger Shaw asks the question: does the state have the right morally, as it has legally, to strip a child of its parent because the parent has offended, although the crime may have been less harmful to the victim than imprisonment of the offender is to her child? I noted in the previous chapter that vicarious punishment was not allowed, but there is a sense in which prisoners' families suffer vicariously.

At any given time many, if not the majority, of prisoners will be on remand, and thus innocent until proven guilty. There will be some prisoners who are wrongly convicted, who are innocent. A whole string of quashed convictions in recent years reminds us of this truth. Again, many will not be wicked, but feckless or inadequate. The prison governor Andrew Coyle writes that when he first went into Edinburgh prison, he

> understood what was meant by the description of prisons as the dustbins of society. Regimented in rows were broken men, with sallow faces and sunken eyes, clinging to their humanity; those who could not cope; those to whom society had given the label of failure. For them prison was the ultimate asylum, the last place of safety. (Coyle, 1994, p. 32)

Prisoners, especially remand prisoners, will also have a statistically high risk of committing suicide. In Britain in 2002, 94 people committed suicide in prison, 6 in one prison alone, one of whom was a mother of three young children who had acted as a drug courier because of the desperation of poverty.

The prisons

Howard's reports of prisons which were dens of vice and corruption, insanitary, with rats which could eat you alive and more people dying of typhus and 'jail fever' than were sent to the gallows, galvanized the consciences of Europe. New prisons were built but, given the prevailing enthusiasm for neo-Gothic, it is not surprising that many of them opted for 'Gothic terror'. Outside and inside these prisons approximated the image of a medieval dungeon. They were built to express disapproval and as vehicles for penitential suffering. All over Britain these prisons still preach their message. A *Guardian* reporter in 1960 said of one of them, Armley Jail in Leeds: 'In all England, I saw no comparably resounding statement of man's persisting determination to render evil for evil.' At the same time aspects were taken over from monastic practices. Like the monk the prisoner had a 'cell' and, like him, was meant to spend time in silence and contemplation.

Pentonville, which was built in 1842, was the model for many later British prisons, and was built on the radial system. The architecture was supposed to express severe disapproval of wrongdoing. More than fifty prisons were built according to this model. It opted for the silent system in which prisoners were supposed to find time to repent. The result was that fifteen or so prisoners each year were sent to the asylum.

In England between 1908 and 1958 prison numbers were reduced and maintained at a low level. Prison building began again in 1959, following which more than twenty prisons were built on a T- or L-shaped plan based on the principle of small housing units with corridors not very different, as it happens, from the undergraduate accommodation built at the time! At this time there was no prison overcrowding. When this again became a problem because of the great incarceration another twenty prisons were built between 1980 and 1996, adding 11,285 places. By 1994 there was overcrowding again and more prisons are being built, two by the private sector, which presents the disagreeable spectacle of punishment becoming a commercial opportunity. The prisoner-to-staff ratio had risen from 7.5:1 in 1947 to 1.5:1 in 1994.

What the architectural rhetoric of the new prisons is remains to be seen. It is now generally agreed they should be small, with not more than 400 inmates, community-based, with light interiors. The emphasis should be on hope rather than suffering. Even the best prisons are, however, in the view of an experienced prison visitor and someone who has experienced prison as a result of anti-nuclear protest, 'terrible places'. 'No matter how they are dressed up, modernised or staffed by well-meaning people there is not a single prison in Britain that we can or should be proud of. Indeed, we should ask forgiveness of everyone there' (Forrester, 1994, p. 63).

Prison as punishment

Since imprisonment became the general form of punishment there have been arguments about whether deprivation of freedom is sufficient punishment, or whether prisons should be made punitive places. At the beginning of the nineteenth century the Anglican clergyman and wit Sydney Smith believed that 'in prisons . . . there must be a great deal of solitude; coarse food; a dress of shame; hard incessant, irksome, eternal labour; a planned and regulated and unrelenting exclusion of happiness'. It is worth asking, and not just ironically, how he derived this view from his Scriptures. By the end of the century, and for the first half of the twentieth, it was generally agreed, to the contrary, that prisoners are sent to prison *as* a punishment not *for* punishment but 'the pain of imprisonment' remains, which includes not just the loss of perhaps years of one's life, but deprivation of relationships with family, with members of the opposite sex, of freedom to do what one wants. Beyond that, in the new incarceration some prisons in the United States are described as 'life trashing'. The State of Georgia has abandoned rehabilitation. Gym activities have been curtailed, hot lunch done away with, prisoners compelled to call staff 'Sir' or 'Ma'am'.

In Britain prison conditions have been attacked by reformers since the nineteenth century. In 1980 the then Director of the Prison Department described the conditions in some institutions as 'an affront to civilized society'. Since then attempts to improve have certainly been made, and the prison service insists that there are no gratuitous punishments in them, that food, clothing and hygiene have been normalized and that the sepulchral atmosphere has been lifted. On the other hand prisoners continue to speak of deprivation and degradation and one can see why. Prisoners have numbers rather than names, they have standardized clothing, little personal space and no responsibility. Others decide when the prisoner can leave his or her cell, shower, exercise, eat, and so on. The focus is on obedience and learning to take orders. Humiliation, that is to say, is still part of the nature of prison experience. Just as violence breeds violence, so humiliation breeds contempt. Prisons can only be constructive if prisoners are recognized as people of worth, and if their self-respect is increased.

So, too, is brutality and racism. It is alleged that homosexual rape is common, a product of sexual deprivation and frustration and also a means of degradation. Punishments are targeted disproportionately against ethnic groups. Racist victimization in prison is a common occurrence. If a poor sense of self-worth contributes to crime then prison exacerbates this.

Power hierarchies are found within prisons as in any institution. One of the reasons why most prisoners are keen that order should be maintained is that disturbances provide opportunities to settle scores and confirm moral hierarchies. In his report on the riots at Strangeways Prison in Manchester in 1990 Lord Woolf emphasized the need for justice in prison, by which he meant the observance of basic human rights, the provision of adequate food, medical care and respect for human dignity. He felt that the main problem in the prison system was the unsatisfactory state of relationships. In São Paulo in Brazil a Christian group, the Association for the Protection and Assistance of the Convicted (APAC), took over a small local prison where order had broken down and regenerated it on the basis of good relationships, relationships of respect, between all members of the prison community. Prisoners are called *recuperandos*, those recovering, and the task of prison is seen to be to learn to relate positively both with other inmates and also with family outside, until release is possible. Their policy is that families should live not more than ten miles from the prison, that daily phone calls should be possible and that in the later stages of a sentence they should visit daily.

Prisons as defence and deterrence

It is generally agreed that there are some offenders who have to be detained for public safety. In England and Wales this only amounts to a few hundred prisoners (578 in 1993) and a few thousand more in category B (5,149 in 1993). At best this is one-tenth of the overall prison population. Most prisoners are no danger to anyone but themselves. If the statistics about types of crime are right the defence argument is no justification for the imprisonment of most people, and certainly most women, in British jails.

A second justification of imprisonment is that it deters individuals and others from committing offences. The 'prison works' dogma was a response to the 'nothing works' pessimism of the early 1970s. That earlier pessimism, however, was based partly on a huge amount of evidence that high imprisonment rates do not deter crime, and that evidence remains valid.

Does prison 'work' in the sense that it deters would-be offenders and protects society from established ones? Prisons are costly. Today it is calculated that it costs between £20,000 and £37,000 to keep a prisoner in jail for a year, more than enough to send them to public school. Prisons are overcrowded in spite of the huge building programme. Above all they are a conspicuous failure in terms of the subsequent behaviour of those committed to them. Around three-quarters of young offenders and half of all offenders commit another crime within two years of release. On the day that the millionaire Lord Archer was released from prison a number of newspapers followed the fortunes of other prisoners released at the same time. Lord Archer went to his country mansion. One young offender left prison with £3.60 in his pocket, no change of clothes and no home to go to. The reporter bought him a meal and a bus ticket. Without that, he said, he would certainly have stolen just to get food. It can also be argued that prisons are of marginal value in terms of public protection because so small a proportion of those responsible are caught, convicted and imprisoned.

The claim that 'prison works' in terms of deterrence is also contradicted by comparative figures of crime and imprisonment from society to society. The imprisonment rate in the United States is six times that of Britain while the homicide rate is seven times that of Switzerland which has 40 per cent less imprisonment than Britain and widespread gun ownership. Between 1987 and 1995 the United States increased its prison population by 124 per cent and achieved a 2 per cent increase in crime; Denmark increased its prison population by 7 per cent and had a 3 per cent increase in crime. Denmark has a low incarceration rate and a low crime rate while the United States has a high incarceration rate, a high risk rate, and a high crime rate. As Jock Young ironically remarks, one would expect plane loads of Congressmen to be flying to Denmark to learn the secret of success. The truth is, of course, that crime rates have very little to do with the risk of being imprisoned and much more to do with other factors such as the cohesiveness of the community.

Prison as penitentiary

In the United States prisons are still known as 'penitentiaries', a name which signifies their existence for rehabilitation. As we saw, the idea of reform or rehabilitation was part of the ideology of prison very early on, and it shared attributes of the Protestant work ethic: the redemptive significance of work, the importance of education, the need for moral influence and the importance of discipline. This understanding of the prison is challenged even by sympathetic prison governors like Andrew Coyle who describe it as 'at best patronizing and at worst arrogant' on the grounds that it assumes that it is possible for one group of human beings to impose personal change on another human group. Rehabilitation means rejoining those citizens who agree to be normed by law and this, Coyle and others argue, is not something one can be forced to do but something which must be chosen.

It can also be argued that prison has never rehabilitated people in practice. Clemner in 1940 wrote about 'prisonization', the gradual destructive socialization of prisoners into the norms of prison life which makes it difficult for them successfully to adapt to a law-abiding life outside, thereby possibly deepening criminality. As prisons in fact exist, at least in Britain, then, remarks Duff, they could not be described as rehabilitative without 'callous irony'. It is true that the present government is putting more emphasis on constructive regimes in prison but, according to the Prison Inspector's Report in 1998, still not enough. And of course, there is nothing rehabilitative about a two-week sentence. This is intended as a 'short, sharp shock' and perhaps it does so work for some offenders, but at what cost to society and to the individual's family?

Nevertheless it is surely the case that rehabilitation cannot be written out of the meaning of prisons. Woolf recommended that incentives should be built into the prison system to create a clear sense of progress through the course of a sentence. The third of the British government's goals for the prison service is 'to develop constructive regimes'. Among the goals of the Prison Agency set up in 1993 are these: prisons should 'provide positive regimes which help prisoners address their offending behaviour and allow them as full and responsible a life as possible and should help prisoners prepare for their return to community'. These goals are rehabilitative, and indeed institutions which existed purely for restraint or for punishment would not be moral places. Prison ought to serve the public not just by keeping people in custody but by preventing crime. If prisoners are released in an embittered and disaffected state this does not happen. This means that prisons need to be places where hope is engendered. As Paul understood, hope is impossible without faith, and here specifically faith in the possibilities of every prisoner.

At the same time it can be argued that removing people from the community is the very last thing we want if we want to reintegrate offenders. When young offenders return to the community after a spell in prison, vital links with others of their own age, relationships with adults and a job to go to are often missing. In Britain community sentencing has an 11 per cent better record in terms of re-offending, conceivably because the links with the community are not broken. As we shall see in Chapter 8, some criminologists have argued that shame and reintegration are the real stuff of crime control, and that therefore imprisonment is completely misguided. Prisons, as Andrew Coyle's remarks seem to indicate, are warehouses for outcasts. Far from helping to reintegrate people they foster participation in criminal subcultures. George Bernard Shaw noted that the prison authorities 'profess three objects: (a) Retribution (a euphemism for vengeance), (b) Deterrence (a euphemism for Terrorism) and (c) Reform . . . They achieve the first atrociously. They fail in the second . . . the third is irreconcilable with the first.' Soaring prison numbers in the face of the proved failure of prisons to either deter or rehabilitate indicates that the real reason for imprisonment is retribution. These record numbers are a high-water mark of the punitiveness of our societies, a marker, in fact, of their scapegoating tendencies.

The prisoner as scapegoat

Scapegoat theory has been largely developed over the past forty years by the French cultural anthropologist René Girard. Girard's thesis is simple. He appeals to Aristotle for the insight that all learning happens through mimesis. To learn as a human being is to imitate others. The problem with imitation is that we all want the same thing, and this generates violence. The story of Cain and Abel is a classic story of two brothers in competition for the same goods (a 'blessing', i.e. success in their enterprise), where the failure of one leads to murder. But mimesis does not just belong to ancient myths or to childhood. The nuclear arms race was a classic instance of mimetic violence while mimesis is one of the major motors of capitalism. As Tony Reilly, chief executive of Heinz, once said: 'Once something is on TV it turns out that everyone wants more or less the same thing.' But as we also know, capitalism presupposes competition, and even, as we often say, 'cut-throat competition', violence.

Before the advent of law, and social conventions, Girard believes we have the war of all against all, as everyone competes for the goods everyone desires. In order to survive, societies have to find a way of limiting violence. This is the scapegoat mechanism. Society channels all its pent-up frustration, anger, rage and aggression on to one single victim – the scapegoat. In the scapegoat ritual outlined in Leviticus 16 the priest lays his hands on the head of a live goat and confesses over it all the people's sins and transgressions, 'putting them on the head of the goat'. The goat is then driven into the wilderness, bearing the people's iniquities away (Lev 16.21). It is a symbolic story of immense power.

Nothing is said in Leviticus about the role of the whole community in driving away the goat by throwing stones, though this is what happens when people are executed by stoning. Also, the goat is not killed, but simply driven into the wilderness. Girard, however, works on the assumption that the scapegoat is normally killed, and he is able to give copious examples from both Scripture and other world literature to support his case. He also illustrates, only too plausibly, how the scapegoat mechanism has functioned in world history. In European history, for example, the Jews were scapegoated, as were old women (so-called 'witches'), and as are now ethnic minorities. We also know that scapegoating frequently happens within families, or other smaller communities. The scapegoat mechanism, in fact, as is already clear in Leviticus, is a way of dealing with guilt. When we feel guilty, doubt and anger is directed at ourselves: if we cannot deal with that the obvious thing is to displace it on to another. On this other is dumped all of our rage and aggression. That one is the guilty one, guilty of everything. The rhetoric of Isaiah 53 picks this up: 'The LORD has laid on him the iniquity of us all' (Is 53.6). In this way the scapegoat – a person, or a community, or perhaps a symbolic animal – actually saves us or delivers us from our own inner conflict, at least for a time. Girard envisages a situation in primitive society where it was repeated yearly, as, of course, Leviticus envisages. Once the murder has taken place the scapegoat can even become a divine figure since it delivers the person or community from its own anger.

But while the scapegoat mechanism *delivers* from violence, at the same time it *institutionalizes* it as a way of dealing with conflict. This aggression is not absent from law. To be sure, law comes in to control the blood feud and the lynch mob, but the sentiments of retributive justice – make the punishment fit the crime – cast a cool and rational veil over the scapegoat mechanism.

The mechanism of scapegoating is a way of dealing with aggression by aggression. But this is true of retributive justice also which may be a way of scapegoating others. Girard has illustrated how the Jews were scapegoated in medieval Europe. In the early modern period attention switched to vagabonds, vagrants, masterless men, the poor. Between 1690 and 1850 these were hanged, transported, flogged and imprisoned in quite astonishing numbers. Society was changing with breathless speed. People were desperately uneasy about the consequences: they sought and found a scapegoat.

The architecture of British jails is the architecture of the scapegoat. These huge structures are a 'wilderness' of bars and keys. Prisons are part of the community, but much prison architecture exists to deny that: in the rhetoric of concrete, razor wire and stone it says: those within have forfeited their right to be considered part of community. Small wonder that anywhere there is a prison only a handful of citizens know, or want to know, it; only a handful of dedicated souls enter its gates to visit. Those within are those driven out, like the goat for Azazel. They are there to pay the price for all.

Scapegoating works by essentializing and demonizing the other. It involves distancing mechanisms which explain crime in a way which denies that it has any relationship with the core values and structure of society. It manufactures monsters who are beyond redemption and cannot change. To accept the binary – the normal and the monstrous – is to deny the monstrous in all of us, the dark side of our aggression and sexuality.

The Norwegian criminologist Thomas Mathiesen argues that prisons serve a diverting function. As we saw in Chapter 4, most crime is actually committed by the powerful. Those caught by the punishment machine and especially those placed behind bars are very largely traditional criminals from the lower working class. Our attention is diverted. Thus prison has a symbolic function. They are black and we are white. All these functions are ideological.

Shakespeare reflects most insistently on retributive justice in *Measure for Measure* which is a sort of extended meditation on Romans 11.32: 'God has shut up all to disobedience that God might have mercy on all.' It is a passionate exposé of scapegoating logic.

In the play we have a kingdom ruled by a duke (like Prospero, one of Shakespeare's 'God' figures) who is about to leave for a sabbatical. Part of his reason for doing so is that he feels he has administered the laws too laxly, and he wants to see how his virtuous deputy, Angelo, will cope. In fact he does not disappear but only takes disguise as a friar. In New Testament terms, he does not consider his greatness something to be hung on to (Phil 2.6) but is henceforth to be found quite literally in the underworld, visiting 'the spirits in prison' (1 Pet 3.19).

No sooner has the Duke left than the laws against promiscuity are set in force with full vigour. A young man, Claudio, is condemned to death for getting his intended with child. Claudio has a virtuous sister, Isabella, about to take the veil: she is urged by the 'low life' Lucio to plead with Angelo. Eventually Angelo extorts from her a promise that he will spare her brother if she sleeps with him. The Duke knows that Angelo once broke a marriage contract because the dowry promised him was inadequate: in pitch darkness this jilted lady goes to bed with Angelo in place of Isabella. But no sooner has Angelo had his pleasure than he sends a peremptory note for the execution of Claudio. Down in the condemned cells the Duke at first suggests a notorious criminal, Barnadine, be executed in Claudio's stead, but he is too drunk, 'unfit to live or die'. The convenient death from fever of another prisoner solves this dilemma. But soon comes the denouement: the Duke gives up his disguise, and all is made plain. The spirits in prison are delivered, including even Barnadine. All are judged, and all receive mercy.

Puritan societies are notoriously punitive societies. In Puritan England Shakespeare gives his own assessment of criminal justice, of the relation between the underworld – pimps, bawds, welfare scroungers – and the overworld – government, and even the virtuous Isabella. For the most chilling line in the play is hers, 'more than my brother is my chastity'. At the end of the play the Duke acknowledges *his* need, in asking for her hand in marriage, and she gives up her deadly principle. Angelo has proposed a logic of violence, making an example of the young and incautious and the loose-living. Claudio was to be made a scapegoat. Why? Clearly because he embodied all those repressed instincts Angelo could not face up to. Shakespeare shows the hypocrisy of this strategy: unmasking it is a prelude to the establishment of a society built upon a different logic, that of forgiveness – one of his favourite themes.

Prison and the community

The whole point of the scapegoat mechanism is to enable society to feel comfortable about itself, to pretend that crime does not belong in the community. Prison is a mechanism for doing that. David Garland remarks that a society which feels morally comfortable about sending thousands of terrified young men and women to institutions in which they are bashed, raped and brutalized, stripped of human dignity, denied freedom of speech and movement, has a doubtful commitment to freedom. From this perspective the penal politics of the past twenty years ought to be a cause for alarm. The huge rise in imprisonment cannot be explained by crime rates, demographic factors or levels of economic activity. It is a matter of political choice. At the end of five years' work as Chief Inspector of

Prisons, Sir David Ramsbotham commented that he had never received ministerial acknowledgement of, or response to, any of his reports or their contents or their recommendations. This is a profound comment on the political opportunism which lies behind penal policy. At the same time, in a democracy, this means that prisons exist because society wants them to. In turn what needs to be explained is the present punitive mood. Mathiesen argues that television, with all its emphasis on sensationalism and scary stories about crime, is one important condition fostering prison growth. Politicians and other decision-makers are obliged to react to the imagery created by the mass media and play their cards accordingly.

Prisons cannot be justified in terms of either deterrence or reform. They have a role in incapacitation, but only for a small number of offenders. What Mathiesen calls 'the fiasco of prison' rationally requires a radical contraction. Scapegoating is a false solution. What is needed is shalom, social inclusion, good work, better education, and the addressing of inequality. Shalom also includes a frank recognition that offenders are a part of the community and that therefore the walls of the prison should be permeable. Woolf recommended that prisoners should be helped to maintain links with their families through having more home visits and by being placed in community prisons as near their homes as possible. The current state of overcrowding makes this impossible, especially for women, for whom there are fewer prisons. Prisons are part of the community. Part of the force of the doctrine of original sin is that we are all responsible for the evil that happens among us. Jesus' term for those who pretended that was not the case was 'whited sepulchres'. At the moment the security culture makes it exceptionally difficult for ordinary members of the public either to learn about or to visit prisons, and one can imagine the hilarity if it was proposed that jails should have regular 'open days' when this was possible. But why not? And how else is integration between prison and community to be achieved? The answer to 'why not' of course is, in part, 'prison culture', but also the stress which prison staff are under because of overcrowding. We are back, once again, to political imperatives, but before we blame politicians let us remember that in a democracy these are our imperatives. As a society we have to ask what kind of prisons we want.

7 | Victims and Offenders

If Scripture can be regarded as dealing centrally with offenders and offences, by the same token it can be seen as centrally concerned with the victim. I want to begin by looking at four of these scriptural stories.

Miroslav Volf offers us a rich exegesis of a story we have touched on already, that of Cain and Abel (Volf, 1999). He begins from an exposition which argues that Cain kills his brother because he has been excluded. God is to blame for Abel's murder because he excluded Cain in the first place. This, says Volf, is exactly what we would expect from our culture: we refuse to take the blame and we think in terms of good and bad, victim and offender. In fact the Old Testament scholar Claus Westermann had long ago pointed out that every human being is potentially both Cain and Abel. We may all be Cain in relation to our neighbour. In different aspects and at different junctures of our lives, suggests Volf, we are both innocent victims and guilty perpetrators. In our innocence we should not forget our sinfulness and in our sense of endangerment we should remember to fear our own dark shadows. In any case, a close reading of the story suggests a different reading. Cain was an agriculturalist and Abel a pastoralist. Perhaps Cain was the big man in the story and God accepts the offering of the poor man. Cain cannot understand that God should prefer a 'nobody' and turns his anger against both God and his brother. Cain persuades himself that his brother should die and chooses a spot outside the public sphere where no help can be procured and no communal judgement can be passed. When challenged he denies both his guilt and his responsibility. By excluding he excludes himself from all relationships. Because belonging is home, and home is a brother who is no more, he becomes a vagrant. Cain, the anti-type who murdered his brother, will be healed by Christ, the type who laid down his life for us, though this requires that Cain walks in Christ's way.

Later in Genesis we have another victim story, that of Joseph, a story which makes the connection between justice and shalom.

Again the story starts with jealousy and the story makes clear that he is a victim who, by his arrogant behaviour, attracted the crime. Joseph is sent to ask after the shalom of his brothers (Gen 37.14) but his behaviour has breached the shalom of the family. His brothers decide first to murder him and then to sell him into slavery. He is a victim of what today would be called 'people trafficking'. The story is ambivalent at this point because on the one hand the intercession by Reuben and Judah is depicted as an attempt to avert the crime of murder, but on the other hand slavery is the condition from which God rescues Israel, the paradigm of the state which God does not will for human beings. The story unfolds through Joseph's rise to power in Egypt and the embassy of the brothers, representing their starving people, to come and buy food, in the course of which Joseph enquires about the shalom of his father. Finally comes the great recognition scene:

> Then Joseph said to his brothers . . . 'I am your brother Joseph, whom you sold into Egypt. And now do not be distressed, or angry with yourselves, because you sold me here; for God sent me before you to preserve life . . . it was not you who sent me here, but God. (Gen 45.4–5, 8)

Here the victim becomes the victor, the powerless occupies the place of power but, at the end, 'pardon's the word for all' because Joseph, or the narrator, recognizes the hand of God behind events, turning sin, or crime, into blessing. Shalom is re-established. Justice and peace kiss each other.

This victim story is taken up in the way the Church has understood the crucifixion. It is the earliest version of the *O felix culpa* – O happy fault which merited such, and so great, a redemption.

A very different story is that of the Levite's concubine in Judges 19. The story is told in a leisurely way, with much narrative detail which is not immediately relevant to the outcome. A man from a remote part of the country takes a concubine from Bethlehem. We are told that there was 'no king in Israel' and it could be that it is the perspective of this narrator that the terrible events which unfold are the dark side of that period, a period of virtual anarchy with no central authority. He and his concubine do not get on and she returns to her father's house for four months, at the end of which time the man goes to fetch her again. On the journey home they end up in Gibeah, where the men of the city pound on the door wanting to commit homosexual rape. His host offers both his daughter and the concubine but finally only the concubine is turned over to the men, who gang rape her all night. It is not clear from the story whether she is dead, or just terribly injured (the Greek translation tells us she was dead, but the Hebrew does not). He takes her home, cuts her in twelve pieces, and sends the parts to each tribe to summon the tribes against the men of Gibeah. Phyllis Trible comments:

> Of all the characters in Scripture, she is the least. Appearing at the beginning and close of a story that rapes her, she is alone in a world of men. Neither the other characters nor the narrator recognizes her humanity. She is property, object, tool, and literary device. Without name, speech, or power, she has no friends to aid her in life or mourn her in death. (Trible, 1984, p. 80)

As the story goes on the Levite excuses himself, putting his own story in the best light, passing over his cowardice, callousness and the possible murder of his concubine. The tribes of Israel make war against Gibeah, slaughter the whole tribe of Benjamin barring six hundred men, and then have to slaughter and abduct six hundred women from Jabesh Gilead and Shiloh so that the tribe can continue. The story is unremittingly dark. Only the opening chapter of 1 Samuel, and the book of Ruth, suggest that women could be treated in a different way. The narrator obviously wants us to take from the story the need for law and order. Trible takes from it the continuance of misogyny and the command to repent. In the context of reflection on the victim we note the way in which the victim can disappear from the narrative altogether, become incidental, a mere trigger for the larger action. And perhaps this is also what the narrator had in mind. Perhaps, with a dark irony, the story does make the point of the anonymity of the victim.

Tellingly, in her exegesis of the story, Trible alludes to Isaiah 53.7: 'Like a lamb that is led to the slaughter, and like a sheep that before its shearers is silent, so he did not open his mouth.' Like the concubine the figure we know as 'the suffering servant' is anonymous. Some suggest it stands for Israel as a whole but this is an implausible reading of Isaiah 53. This figure is 'despised and rejected by others; a man of suffering and acquainted with infirmity'. Is he a victim? He was 'wounded for our transgressions, crushed for our iniquities . . . By a perversion of justice he was taken away. Who could have imagined his future?' It certainly sounds like it. His suffering however, unlike the concubine's, is read as redemptive:

> Upon him was the punishment that made us whole,
> And by his bruises we are healed . . .
> He bore the sin of many
> and made intercession for the transgressors.
>
> (Is 53.5, 12)

Whether or not Isaiah 53 was used by Jesus himself, or by the New Testament community to understand the significance of his story, there is no doubt that Jesus was an innocent victim, crucified for no crime. The New Testament is premised on the claim that his life and death, far from being simply a tragedy, is in fact redemptive. As with the Joseph story, victim status is not a purely negative category but has redemptive significance for the whole community. If Isaiah 53 is our lens, then the suffering of the victim is vicarious. I noted in Chapter 5 that vicarious punishment was no longer considered moral. Perhaps that is because of the priority of autonomy as an ethical category since the eighteenth century, and especially since Kant. The very category of vicariousness, by contrast, implies that the life of each is bound up with the life of all, that the very idea of an autonomous individual is a rationalist fiction, implying some kind of monster who is not conceived and born, not brought up and socialized, and who is absolutely self-sufficient for all his or her needs. Of course, there is no such creature. All of us are, as Kant's contemporary, Schleiermacher, noted, radically dependent. This is true for our basic needs, but also morally, for good and for ill. It is possible, of course, to make a stand against an unjust society, as Chomsky does today in the United States, and as many did in apartheid South Africa. What we cannot do is pretend that we are not part of the society in which we live. Moral isolation is an impossibility. Perhaps vicariousness is the category we need, then, for the conscious decision to live for others rather than to give priority solely to our own agenda. What is odd about the vicarious role of the victim is that it implies the creative use of something forced upon us, for the very idea of victimhood is passive. The victim, as

Isaiah 53 implies, was originally the sacrificial animal, ritually slaughtered and offered in sacrifice. Sacrifice, we know, was not always propitiatory, or expiatory, but sometimes it was. The idea of the vicarious role of the victim seems to follow from here.

For medieval theology the idea of Christ as victim was a major category. The first stanza of 'Sing my tongue the glorious battle' ends:

> Tell how Christ, the world's Redeemer,
> As a Victim won the day.

Victimhood here stands for Christ's willing assumption of sacrifice. The danger with such a theology was that it could evoke a mysticism of suffering which understood pain as something positive, an identification with the crucified Christ. We find this in fourteenth- and fifteenth-century mysticism but also in the mysticism of the poor. The liberation theologians have recorded how such a theology could breed a passive and masochistic acceptance of suffering. In this connection the comment of Cardinal Ratzinger that what was needed in response to the thousands of victims of terror in Latin America was not liberation but a theology of martyrdom is quite scandalous. It misses altogether the dimension of shalom as something towards which we aspire here and now.

A quite different theology of the victim emerged from reflection on the victims of the Holocaust. Most patristic and medieval theology concentrates on human sin, and on Christ's death as the payment for that sin. Reflecting on accounts of Auschwitz like that of Elie Wiesel's *Night*, Jürgen Moltmann (1974) concentrated on the victim. Where was God when 6 million died? Moltmann argued that in dying as a victim God in Christ puts Godself alongside the victims of history. Because the history of Christ is at the same time part of the history of God his death is not just another statistic but offers the hope that the torturers and murderers will not be victors after all. Victims are put under the protection of God and, though lacking human rights here and now, have rights with God. The death of Christ offers hope to the victim eschatologically, but this hope is potent even now, rescuing us from the darkness of despair. This theology understands the cross not through sacrificial theory, but as lying at the heart of the ongoing life of the Triune God, open to history, open to vulnerability, actively seeking the salvation of the godless and godforsaken.

From these biblical and theological reflections on the victim I want to turn to the victim of crime today and see to what extent, if any, they can illumine our understanding of the facts.

Victims of contemporary crime

Street crime, we saw, is probably not the most significant form of crime, even though it is the form of crime for which most people are sent to prison. There are far more victims of suite crime – ranging from people who have lost their pensions, to lung cancer victims, to the victims of the thalidomide drug – and of state crime, than there are of street crime. In the case of state crime we can think, in the twentieth century, of the Armenian, Nazi and Cambodian genocides and of the many less comprehensive forms of ethnic cleansing, including Israeli occupation of the West Bank. We can think of the Soviet purges, the creation of the original gulag, the decimation of the kulaks. Other state crimes, like the bombing of Dresden, Vietnam or Cambodia, go unrepented, their victims, like the Levite's concubine, scarcely acknowledged. The new sub-discipline of 'victimology' has some important things to say about victims, but almost all in relation to street crime, and it needs to be set against this wider context. Furthermore, victims of street crime are also often victims of commercial crime or of other forms of suite crime, a fact often not taken into consideration in reflection on the experience of victims.

Today we are familiar with the annual crime reports which governments simultaneously need to play up and to play down. On the one hand they have to show us they are tackling crime, and that the figures are better than last year. On the other hand they have to show us that expenditure on law and order is justified. Such reports do not consist of neutral data, but are politically freighted, especially when elections are in the offing. In Britain there is an ongoing debate about how they should be read, and dramatic rises and falls in crime are usually to do with what categories of offence are included. On the surface these reports suggest that we live in desperately dangerous societies in which everyone is likely to be a victim. The US Crime Report for 1995, for example, claims that one murder takes place every 24 minutes, one rape every 5 minutes, one robbery every 54 seconds, one aggravated assault every 18 seconds. In that year it is estimated that 35 million Americans were victims of crime. From the British Crime Survey 2001/2 come the statistics that in

Britain there were more than 2.5 million violent crimes, in a population of 60 million; 72 per cent of these were common assaults. There
were nearly half a million cases of domestic violence, 770,000 cases
of acquaintance violence, 992,000 cases of stranger violence and
312,000 muggings. There were also 61,000 rapes, an average of 167 a
day which means that 1 in 20 women are victims. Overall, the risk
of being a victim is 1 in 25. Whereas there were half a million crimes
per annum in 1950 (with half the present population) there are now
over 5 million. These figures are, of course, alarming but, like all statistics, they run the risk of what some statisticians call 'the Judas
factor': Jesus was betrayed by 8 per cent of the disciples! Crime, we
are told, has increased at the rate of 5.1 per cent per annum since
1918 but this certainly does not mean we are 5.1 per cent a year
more in danger of crime.

It is true that street crime is threatening and impacts disproportionately on society as a whole. A number of high-profile child murders in
Britain have affected not just the victims but the entire community so
that parents are no longer happy to allow their children to 'run out
and play'. Children in turn lose the freedom to be children. In the
same way a culture where it was once normal and acceptable to hitch-
hike has been replaced by one where the hitchhiker, especially if he is
a single male, is looked on with profound distrust. A friendly offer of a
lift to an unknown person at a bus stop will probably be viewed as
attempted abduction! A simple way of socializing transport is thereby
forgone. The victim is 'everyman' in a way which the criminal is not.
Eighteenth-century Christians like Howard said of the criminal, 'There
but for the grace of God, go I.' Today the criminal is the demonic
other, with whom we cannot identify. The victim is the one with
whom we identify, an identification which carries with it the implicit
assumption that we are guiltless.

Everybody recognizes that there are genuine victims of street
crime. The impact of murder by strangers, especially of children, is
one that everyone can understand and which everyone fears. Every
time it happens the victim's family, victims themselves, say, 'We
never thought it could happen to us.' Every time, the same cliché is
used: 'the ultimate nightmare', but clichés are sometimes true. At
the same time we have to remember that the incidence of these
crimes is, in Britain and Europe at least, very small. In the literature
of victimology, especially that emanating from North America, there
seems to be a generalization out from these experiences to every

other type of crime, especially property crime. Even in Britain when we had a cycle stolen from the house we were duly sent a victim support card! Of the serious crimes like rape, assault and murder it is true that such experiences disorient our world and remove our sense of being in control of our own lives and destinies. To apply such language to the experience of crime in general is to cheapen it. There is a rather distasteful sense of middle-class hysteria about some of the victim literature. In Britain the 'Victim's Charter' was launched by the Major government, the same government which sought to criminalize begging and drive homeless people from the streets. Such people were clearly not seen as victims; on the contrary, those from whom they begged thought they were. It seems important to distinguish rather sharply between crimes of violence and property crime. It is of course true that property crime against vulnerable people, for example elderly people living alone, can have a quite disproportionate effect on their well-being and it is true that losing articles of great sentimental value, like engagement rings or wedding rings, is very distressing. Property crime in general, however, is never so shocking as violence against the person, where the language of disrespect is properly invoked. As the story of the Levite's concubine makes vividly clear, violent crime treats us as an object, a thing. Violent assault can leave one feeling frightened, vulnerable and defenceless. It carries with it an implication of absolute disrespect for the person which does call into question our sense of living in an ordered world. With respect to property crime, which forms the vast bulk of street crime, it seems to me that claims of loss of autonomy and of having one's entire world shattered are easily exaggerated. The British Crime Survey found that 84 per cent of people who were burgled were affected emotionally, and it is true (I speak as a 'victim') that it makes us feel less secure when we go to bed at night. On the other hand the present debate in Britain, around a farmer who shot dead his 16-year-old burglar, and who is widely supported by the tabloid press for having done so, suggests that we can easily fetishize property, putting its 'rights' above that of human life. And to recall the larger context again, the countries from which these victim surveys emanate have no qualms about selling arms to fuel 'low-intensity conflicts', no qualms about training torturers to use electric prods on the genitals of those who do not believe in the free market, no qualms about dropping four-and-a-half-thousand-pound bombs on troops supporting governments they dislike, and no qualms about pharmaceutical companies refusing to make cheap medication available to developing countries. When we reflect on victims and on crime we are hopelessly blinkered if we avoid these questions.

Who are the victims?

The victims movement has been, in large part, a middle-class movement which flourishes on the back of the perception that we are all victims of crime. Victims' rights are part and parcel of my right to live where I choose, use as much energy as I choose, take my holidays where I choose and so on. When we look at who the victims of crime are in North American and European societies we find, unsurprisingly, that offenders and victims largely come from the same community. The risk of victimization by street crime is linked to age, class, gender, race and area, as well as lifestyle. Age is one of the strongest correlates of victimization and young men between 16 and 24 are most at risk from violent assault. Victims of hate crime also tend to be under 21 while offenders tend to be even younger than their victims. People over 65 are victimized far less than younger ones.

Men are victims in 64 per cent of muggings and 80 per cent of stranger assaults; women are victims of 74 per cent of domestic violence. Unemployed, single people and single parents, followed by those living in the private rented sector and those visiting a pub or club three or more times a week, are also liable to be victims of street crime.

Race and class are also strong indicators: as income goes up, risk goes down. In Britain residents of the poorest council estates have the highest victimization rates. The three most risky areas are mixed inner-metropolitan areas, high-status non-family areas, and the poorest council estates. People in less-well-off council estates are twice as likely to be burgled as those who live in other areas. These areas also have the highest risk for car theft, though just below them are high-status non-family areas.

Afro-Caribbeans and Asians are more at risk than whites, partly because they are over-represented in social and age groups prone to crime and partly because they are most likely to be council tenants or live in socially disadvantaged areas. Black males have the highest rate of victimization.

To some extent it is clear that victims are socially constructed. The women who were once burned as witches are now, properly, considered victims. Should prostitutes be considered as victims? Some argue that they should, but prostitutes' groups themselves have sometimes argued that prostitution may be a legitimate form of labour freely chosen. By the same token some women have argued that one person's rape may be another person's bad night. Perspective clearly has an impact on what we consider to be victimization.

Victims of corporate crimes are treated differently from victims of street crime. If our water is being poisoned by the run-off from farmers using agro-chemicals it makes less sense to say that my autonomy is being denied. As we have seen with many struggles over corporate crime, victims may be faced with a long struggle to gain recognition of their victim status, and finally they may be offered an out-of-court settlement.

The disappearance of the victim

In the Hebrew Bible crimes are dealt with not only by atonement and execution, not only by penal sanction, but also by restitution. In terms of the metaphor of balance, restitution restores the status quo ante. The possibility of restitution was fundamental to much early law. Anglo-Saxon law, for example, allowed offenders to make two payments of compensation for injuries other than homicide: *bot* to the injured party, and *wite* to the lord or king. The word *bot* carries the sense of making better and is related to making amends or penance; *wite* connotes blameworthiness and punishment. This law provided the legal context for Anselm's great essay on the atonement, as 'satisfaction' was the process of making good. A recognized scale of repayments for specific injuries could be invoked and paid to the victim and that would be the end of the matter. There were crimes which were '*bot*-less', for which satisfaction could not be made, and the punishment for those was usually death, but these crimes were the exception. Most crimes, however, were civil torts and the victim was the principal protagonist in court.

The rediscovery of Roman law, and the work of extending and codifying law which went on throughout Europe, changed this situation. The law became professionalized with the emergence of a class of lawyers, and eventually fines, if they were imposed, went not to the victim but to the king. In turn this gave way to deterrence and retribution in the form of physical punishments. The philosophical justification for this was that the wrong done to an individual extends beyond their family to the whole community of which the monarch is the symbolic centre. The end of monarchy as a significant form of rule did not change this situation but intensified it, as the legal profession became more important, and the state took the place of the monarch. In this change, the victim disappeared. In civil cases plaintiffs were still entitled to damages, but in criminal cases they were not. Furthermore, the professionalization of law meant the alienation of the victim, because his or her experience became the substance of abstruse, and sometimes largely unintelligible, legal argument. Victims were summoned to give evidence, and that was that. They were questioned by counsel, but could not tell their own story to the court. They routinely incurred expenses and loss of earnings in addition to what they might have lost from the earlier victimization. From a situation where victims had been at the centre of the legal process, they had moved to the shadowy margins.

The reappearance of the victim and its dangers

The sociologist Norbert Elias talks of a civilizing process which he traces from the end of the European Middle Ages in the course of which manners improve, savage sports like bear baiting, cock fighting (or fox hunting!) disappear, sensibilities become finer and human rights become a central part of the political agenda. In the face of the horrors of the twentieth century it is of course possible to pour scorn on that argument but it is certain that the growth in the consciousness of rights and the accompanying discourse does mark a change in the perception of the person. It is interesting to look at the complaints around 'Gulf War syndrome' associated with the first Gulf War and compare them with what soldiers suffered in the First World War without any complaint or suggestion that the Ministry of Defence should be sued. In the same way trades union and sexual harassment legislation have made forms of behaviour which were once taken for granted completely unacceptable. This change in structures of affect has meant that people are now more conscious of their rights, and this has had effects on the criminal justice process.

One of the markers of change was that victim support groups have sprung up all over the Western world in response to different categories of offence. Specialist groups have been established for victims of particular crimes, such as rape crisis centres, women's refuges and telephone helplines for children, for survivors of incest and homosexual assault. What victims are offered is primarily an expression of concern on behalf of the community and emotional support. Practical help in repairing the damage caused by crime may also be offered when required, for instance in getting repairs done. Increasingly there is a move away from the addressing of needs to the issue of rights, such as the right to be kept informed, and to compensation.

There is much in this which is good and necessary. There is no doubt that victims ought to have a greater role in the criminal justice process, but there are also grounds for concern at the way the process has developed. In the first place, conservative politicians (in the non-party sense) have adopted the cause of crime victims as their own and advocated all kinds of punitive measures as necessary to do justice to the victims. The idea of the victim has been invoked to lever up punitiveness. For penal populism concern for victims is an easy way to political popularity. Sympathy for crime victims can become a cry for vengeance. The battle of good and evil is invoked between the innocent victim and the evil attacker, a battle which is taken up in the 'war on crime'. Victim surveys, however, reveal that victims are no more punitive than the general public and many are willing to engage in direct mediation or receive monetary or other compensation from their offender.

Second, the legitimate demand for rights for the underprivileged and for minorities has been co-opted by the middle class so that we have a culture of complaint which operates adversarially. For those who have the money or know the ropes, taking cases to court, 'being a victim', can pay. Those who reap the benefits of the victims' charter are those who, in social or monetary terms, are the ones who least need it. The last thing anyone thinks of in this culture is forgiveness.

Third, it has been argued that most people hate to think of themselves as victims and that nothing could be more degrading. On the contrary, one has to reply, in the moral power game the cry of 'victim' is one way of guilt-tripping others and thus gaining power over them. In contemporary society we have the spectacle of different groups all claiming to be more victimized than the last, rather like Monty Python's 'Northerners'. Being a victim means we can shed our own responsibility for the way that society is.

Healing victims

Diana Lamplugh, whose 25-year-old daughter disappeared in London, and who was almost certainly murdered, has left a moving account of the experience of the victim's family. She and her husband found, first, that they had no rights. They were sent away from the place where her daughter's car had been found because they were getting in the way. They found that friends had no way of speaking to them, did not know how to deal with the pain. They found themselves unknown participants in a drama which gripped the nation, their daughter's picture on every front page. The Church, too, had no sense of how to deal pastorally with them. In the literature of Holocaust survivors we find something similar: people have no idea how to deal with it. The book of Job is a biblical reflection on this incomprehension of the victim's experience.

Diana Lamplugh writes as the mother of a crime victim. In the many instances of assault each year it is emphasized that victims are rarely purely passive. More than a quarter of all murders, for example, are linked to aggressive behaviour by the victim. In these cases victims did not act to defuse a situation but aggravated it. Factors leading to becoming a victim include exposure (e.g. delivering cash), unwise associations, dangerous behaviours, high-risk activities, and lack of care. Victims are likely to be victimized again. Robbery victims have a nine times greater chance of being attacked again, and sexual assault victims have a thirty-five times greater chance. As noted in the story of Cain and Abel, the roles of victim and offender may be interchangeable. Abused children may grow up to become abusive parents, sexually molested children may become sex offenders, battered wives may kill their spouses, and persons preyed on by stalkers may retaliate.

Victims have to find ways to deal with their experience. It is common for victims to blame themselves, to internalize oppression. Anger is usually part of the experience – anger at the perpetrators, anger at themselves, anger at the system, anger at friends and at God. Victims have to face their vulnerability, their helplessness. They have to find a balance between a false sense of guilt on the one hand and what may be an inappropriate denial of moral responsibility on the other.

What heals the wounds crime inflicts? There seem to be three responses to this question. The first is that victims want to have answers to questions such as 'Why me?', 'What if it happens again?' The British Crime Survey found that the commonest reason for victims to want to meet offenders is to see what they are like or to know why they did it, to give offenders a piece of their mind, to arrange for compensation, or to let offenders see the effect crime had on them. Of victims taking part in mediation 73 per cent wanted an apology, 80 per cent said it was very important to receive answers, and 90 per cent wanted to tell the offender about the impact of the crime. By no means all victims have shown that substantial reparation is what they want most. They often seek symbolic reparation and opportunity to persuade the offender not to offend again.

Diana Lamplugh found healing by throwing herself into work to address violence and aggression in the workplace, personal safety courses and conferences on sex offending. The person who murdered her daughter was never convicted, but there is strong evidence that the person responsible was unstable and had an 'appalling' life before prison. For her a new understanding of resurrection (mediated by a sermon!) opened a pathway for inner healing through forgiveness. She acknowledges that she cannot forgive for her daughter or her other children, but 'I can for myself forgive the part of him who "knows not what he does" and pray that he never again falls to the mercy of that hideous part with the energy which causes such horrendous damage' (Lamplugh, 1997, p. 93). It is doubtful whether it is possible to talk of healing without thus talking of forgiveness. Forgiveness, it has been cogently argued, is not a once-for-all event but a way, a path of discipleship which has to be trodden again and again. Rowan Williams understands the resurrection as an event which heals memories of betrayal and desertion (Williams, 1982). Given the reality of sin and evil we cannot expect pristine purity and wholeness. On the contrary, there is nothing so whole as a broken and healed heart, nothing so complete as a new creation whose fractures have been fully healed. God, he argues, is the 'presence' to which all reality is present and it is this presence which enables memories to be healed.

Beyond forgiveness victims need to know that steps are being taken to prevent the recurrence of the experience. This is essentially what Diana Lamplugh was doing in initiating work to tackle violence. The implication of what she is doing is that we need to work harder to understand violent behaviour and how to tackle it.

Condemnation is not enough. Belief in original sin is no reason for throwing up our hands and explaining violence as an ineradicable part of the human condition. On the contrary, some rehabilitation schemes, like that at Barlinnie (now done away with) and that run by the community prison scheme (APAC) in Brazil, have been notably successful in tackling such behaviour. In Britain one of the most exciting suggestions has been that the procedures of conflict resolution become a standard part of primary education so that children are socialized from the very first to understand both that there are other ways to solve problems than through violence, and to respect and understand the feelings of others. These procedures are being followed today between Muslim and Catholic children in Croatia. Such education might go some way to fill the gap caused by the breakdown of traditional moral structures. These kinds of response to victimization relate to the most difficult of the scriptural victim stories, that of Joseph. Of course, it would be unspeakable to go to any victim of serious crime, or their relatives, and tell them that God would bring good out of evil. It is perhaps the strangest, and yet one of the most consistent, aspects of human experience, however, that this happens, and Christianity places it at the heart of the mystery of redemption. To bring good out of evil is to refuse to allow evil to triumph, to have it all its own way, to let its logic win. It is to defeat it. This is the point of both the Joseph story and the story of Christ. And the stories of the overcoming of evil which I have just cited in different ways all show this happening. In the deepest sense they are redemptive.

Third, where it is possible (which it obviously is not in the case of murder), victims want restitution – not revenge, which is the mirror image of the offence. In this connection something has been done through compensation schemes which address the needs caused by loss of earnings, expenditure incurred because of disablement and pain and suffering. Criminal injuries compensation programmes are a way for society, through the state, to show concern for victims of violence and to enable offenders to make restitution themselves. In 1999 in Britain 43 per cent of offenders sentenced in magistrates' courts for offences of violence, 27 per cent for burglary, 45 per cent for robbery, 31 per cent for fraud and forgery and 51 per cent for criminal damage were ordered to pay compensation. In the Crown Court the figures were much lower, partly because compensation orders are not normally combined with custodial sentences.

Compensation is also made through the state-funded Criminal Injuries Compensation Scheme. Set up in 1964, victim recourse to CICS has increased dramatically from 22,000 claimants in 1979–80 to 78,000 in 1999–2000.

At the end of the day we come back once more to the issue of community, to the creation of shalom. As the most insightful writer on victimology has put it, 'Humaneness is indivisible. The concern for the victim should not obliterate the fact that those who are labelled as criminals are more often than not victims themselves' (Fattah, 1997, p. 268). The primary task of the criminal law is not to punish but, as in ancient Israel, to restore peace, heal injury and redress harm. This brings us to the theme of our next chapter, which is restorative justice.

8 | Justice and Reconciliation

A powerful man happens to catch sight of a beautiful woman naked. It turns out she is married, but, his desires inflamed, he uses his power to seduce her. Unfortunately, she gets pregnant. He does what he can to get the husband to sleep with his wife, but fails. Frightened of getting caught out he has the man killed in what looks like an accident. What ought to happen to the offender? Clearly, he is guilty of both adultery and murder and, in his society, death is the penalty for both. What actually happens is that he is shamed and denounced. For this is, of course, David, King of Israel, the Lord's anointed. What follows his shaming is some kind of process of reintegration. David continues as king. True, his lax morals and his failure to provide adequate parenting for his children do bring down trouble on his head, but his crime is not dealt with by retribution.

Christian societies have frequently been retributive societies, but this suggests they have not understood their origins well enough. In what we call the 'Sermon on the Mount' Jesus proposes that retribution is not the way to deal with offences. On the contrary, he suggests that worship is impossible if we have not first sought reconciliation with our neighbour (Mt 5.24). Paul believes that we have been reconciled to God through the death of Christ and that, in virtue of what Christ has done, we are entrusted with 'a ministry of reconciliation' (Rom 5.10; 2 Cor 5.18). Whoever the author, or authors, of Colossians and Ephesians were they understood reconciliation as at the heart of the gospel message. Through Christ, says Colossians, 'God was pleased to reconcile to himself all things, whether on earth or in heaven, by making peace through the blood of his cross' (Col 1.20). As we saw in Chapter 1, the author of Ephesians insists that Christ is our peace and has initiated a praxis of reconciliation (Eph 2.14–17).

The Hebrew word for 'peace' in these passages is, of course, shalom. Christ is God's shalom, and Christians are accordingly called to peace-making. This, says the author of Ephesians, calls all the operations of the law as we know them into question. The model of justice which is known variously as restorative justice, community justice, or relational justice seeks to build on these insights and it is this which I consider in this chapter. I shall outline its main affirmations, consider the thesis of reintegrative shaming, mediation and reparation, before going on to a consideration of justice and forgiveness.

Restorative justice

In the previous chapter I noted those changes in the legal system which led to the disappearance of the victim. In the course of these changes punishment and retribution took precedence over restitution. Today we simply take it for granted that the sanctions imposed by society will take the form of punishment. That assumption seems to imply in turn that society is basically just, that the threat of punishment is the best way of motivating people to behave well towards each other and that there is a just measure of punishment for each case. As we have seen, all of these assumptions are questionable. They are not effective in deterring crime, they exclude offenders and they do not heal victims. These manifold failures have led people around the world to look to an alternative method of justice which has deep roots in many traditional societies. In the wake of a long and bloody civil war in Papua New Guinea, for example, the Western model of court-administered justice proved futile. The various groups involved went back to traditional models which involved a ritual punishment to satisfy the victim and a public shaming of the offender. After an expression of sorrow and a suitable gift to the victim the offender was reintegrated into the community. They found these practices went further to heal community wounds than retributive justice was able to do.

The United Nations defines restorative justice as a process 'in which the victim, the offender, and/or any other individuals or community members affected by a crime, participate actively together in the resolution of matters arising from the crime'. There are various ways in which this process differs from Western patterns of retributive justice. In the first place justice is the concern of the whole community, and not of legal professionals and a judge who is paid by the state. Injustice, it is recognized, damages the community, but also expresses a damage within the community. Only the community can put this right. It follows from this that justice is not 'administered' in imposing courtrooms where ushers cry 'Pray be upstanding for his Honour the Judge', but in community halls or wherever the community gathers. Minucius Felix said of the early Christians that they needed no shrines or altars. In the same way, restorative justice needs no courts. Second, the process is a palaver, in which everyone can have their say in defence of, or in accusation of, the accused. The victim is not sidelined but is, to the contrary, a prominent player in the whole process. The object is that the victim should have justice done to him or her, rather than justice be meted out to the offender. At the end of the day, however, the desired aim is not to punish whoever the guilty party might be, but to bring healing, reconciliation, shalom, to the community. It is an implication of this process that crime is viewed primarily as a breakdown in relationships rather than as a breach of the law. Justice, in turn, is the restoration of relationship, something which cannot be decreed by statute but only decided by debate and negotiation. The process allows a much more complex understanding of human agency, guilt and responsibility than the conventional justice system which is organized around victim and offender, guilt and innocence.

Perhaps this description sounds a bit starry-eyed and we might ask why the whole legal process as we know it took the place of earlier practices of restorative justice. Was it just a process of consolidation of power by the king and then by the state, or were there real problems in the earlier process? Of course, there were. In the first place the question of power is not absent in any community. One could not imagine restorative justice processes such as these operating between caste Hindus and Dalits, for example. By the same token, would they work in a class society, or even just in a society dominated by the local big family? Surely, state-administered justice delivers us from local tyrannies where violence or the threat of violence lies behind the administration of justice. Furthermore, we should know better than to romanticize traditional communities, which were often highly intolerant of difference and in that sense a model to which we do not wish to return. In such communities individual rights could easily get lost and behaviour perceived to be deviant be cruelly policed. All these objections are correct. The growth of the legal system was not simply malign. It represented an attempt to attain some objectivity over and above the push and pull of influence and community politics.

Second, we might object that even if such processes were desirable the communities which are their essential presupposition no longer exist. Restorative justice methods may be suitable for technologically simple, poor societies with strong informal social control and little mobility but are not appropriate to technologically complex rich societies. Since the beginning of industrialization and the growth of the mega city we have known that there is no going back. The anonymous, privatized society is what we are stuck with and there is no longer a community to administer justice. The idea that cities and suburbs are really networks of villages where community can be mobilized is a pipe dream. There is certainly truth (though not the whole truth) in this objection. Nearer to the truth is the perception that there has never been an ideal community and that every society has tried to find out what is meant by it. We can neither live without it nor live with it as we have it. In contemporary urban society it is not so much a question of subcultures (though of course they exist) as of a tangled skein of overlapping communities to which we have varying degrees of allegiance and through which our humanness is fashioned. We can also respond that restorative justice is close to the theory of communicative action argued for by Habermas and to this extent does not appeal to a traditional model of society but rather to a very sophisticated one. This theory is actually based on a very ancient insight. 'There are certain duties that we owe even to those who have wronged us,' remarked Cicero.

> For there is a limit to retribution and to punishment . . . there are two ways of settling a dispute: first, by discussion; second, by physical force; and since the former is characteristic of man, the latter of the brute, we must resort to force only in the case we may not avail ourselves of discussion. (*On Duties*, Book 1)

Of course Plato had already raised the question of what happens when persuasion becomes force, but in the context of restorative justice we can note that the process of dealing with disputes by argument rather than by force does not just rest on a romantic appeal to a vanished community, but on the contrary appeals to a non-Hobbesian vision of the human, and on a rather sophisticated account of how human societies best function.

Third, it might be objected that if such processes are put in place alongside the existing judicial system they may be felt to constitute 'second-class justice'. Retributivism is bred so deeply into our bones that we might feel that unless just deserts are administered there is no justice. Further, there are a whole series of questions about safeguards: what happens if the victim is vengeful? What happens when the offender is not a member of the community but a stranger? Even in societies where restorative justice was traditional, like Papua New Guinea, punishment remained as a last resort. Before colonization men who regularly killed people from other villages or committed acts likely to lead to war were executed when all else failed.

Fourth, we have to ask whether the labour of jurists from the tenth century on, not to mention the jurists of ancient Greece and Rome, does not have something to teach us, as Luther believed. Does restorative justice offer a coherent view of the rights and responsibilities of the victim, of offenders and the state? How would it deal with suite crime or state crime?

These are all valid questions and the sections which follow, on reintegrative shaming, mediation and reparation seek to explore some of the answers.

Reintegrative shaming

The Australian criminologist John Braithwaite has offered a coherent philosophical and sociological underpinning to restorative processes in his seminal book *Crime, Shame and Reintegration*. Community is at the heart of his concerns. On the one hand he argues that criminal justice should enhance what he calls 'dominion', by which he means individual liberty and freedom from state interference, but on the other hand he opposes individualism. To the objection that that is just the society we have, and we have to live with it, he replies that even in highly urbanized societies people still recognize their mutual interdependence in all sorts of ways, primarily through the family, but also in places of work, churches and the various voluntary groups we are members of. Individualism, then, represents a societal trend which we recognize but which is not fate. We can resist it, and it is important to do so.

It is important because individualism makes it far more difficult to deal with crime. As the title of his book indicates, his basic insight is that crime is best dealt with by a form of shaming which is reintegrative. Braithwaite argues that the process of shaming is the way in which children acquire a moral sense. The process depends on having a family where there are strong relationships and where bad behaviour can be condemned but the child be accepted and loved at the same time. This is reintegrative shaming which, according to the good old Christian motto, hates the sin but loves the sinner. Its goal is forgiveness and acceptance. Where for our society guilt and shame are pathological, to be overcome, for Braithwaite they are proper to our humanness. Guilt is the failure to live up to the standards of one's own conscience and shame is a reaction to criticism by other people, but inducing these feelings is part of the same social process. Families, and by implication communities, with poor relationships are less able to appeal to shame controls. Only in the context of relationships meaningful to the offender can there be an effective shaming and a change of attitude. For adolescents and adults, Braithwaite argues, conscience is a much more powerful weapon to control behaviour than punishment.

Reintegrative shaming works by reinforcing the moral norms. As examples of societies which use it effectively he appeals to the Victorian world, which despite being a period of massive urbanization, industrialization and class conflict saw a decline in crime. He argues that this is because it was a shaming society. There was hypocrisy, but reintegrative shaming is in a considerable measure a policy of hypocrisy; it is a policy of leaving guilty people unpunished, a policy of symbolic shame followed by tangible mercy. He believes that the rise of the rehabilitative ideal was a symptom of a cultural transformation that saw Victorian society refine the power of shaming while increasingly rejecting the principle of casting out. In the contemporary world Japanese society has high interdependence and employs reintegrative shaming. Apology has a central place in the aftermath of Japanese legal conflicts and there are ceremonies of restoration to signify the re-establishment of harmony between conflicting parties. He argues that societies which replace much of their punitive social control with shaming and reintegrative appeals to the better nature of people will be societies with less crime. Punishment and persuasion, on his view, are based on fundamentally different models of human behaviour. Punishment presumes human beings to be rational actors who weigh the benefits of non-compliance against the probability and costs of punishment. Persuasion presumes human beings to be reasonable, of good faith, and motivated to heed advice. Neither model fits all situations.

Shaming has also been shown to work for white-collar crime. Newspaper campaigns which highlight abuses by big corporations stand a better chance of affecting behaviour than legislation. The current view that corporations exist for profit maximization amounts to a denial that they, and individuals acting in corporate roles, are part of a moral community. What is needed in response to this is a return to communitarianism, an assertion of the supremacy of conscience over rational calculation.

The theory of reintegrative shaming implies that rather than be tolerant and understanding we should be intolerant and understanding. We should shame what we do not presently shame while maintaining bonds of communication, affection and respect. Shaming punishes through social disapproval and gossip. These are effective when the targets of shame are not directly confronted with the shame but are directly confronted with gestures of forgiveness or reintegration.

The opposite of this process is disintegrative shaming, in which offenders are condemned and cast out. Disintegrative shaming divides the community by creating a class of outcasts. It helps create criminal subcultures which reject the rejectors. Braithwaite argues that stigmatization is less likely in communitarian cultures because the complex experience that people have of each other makes it more difficult to squeeze the identities of offenders into crude master categories of deviance. He acknowledges that shaming can be a medium for the tyranny of the majority but argues that a society that lacks a capacity to mobilize social disapproval will never guarantee freedom to deviate and will never offer the minority protection from the tyranny of the majority. If it cannot mobilize disapproval it will not be able to exercise control against those who trample on the freedom to be different. He grants that communitarianism is a two-edged sword but believes that the crime-preventing edge is more important than the crime-producing one.

Since Braithwaite advanced this argument (in 1988) the communitarian thesis has been well aired and by and large met with much scepticism. People are evidently not convinced that communitarian societies are well placed to protect supposedly deviant minorities, to promote justice as difference. Even if we wanted them, it might be argued, how would we go about promoting them in societies where mobility is as high as it is in ours, where the average US citizen stays in the same house only for five years?

Braithwaite's model presumes that everyone in the community knows one another, but nothing could be further from the truth. We are a society of strangers, and many people are only too happy to keep it that way. Warnings against gossip in Scripture (Prov 11.9; Jas 3.5–6) remind us that this way of enforcing morality may be malicious and destroy the innocent. On both counts it seems that his view of human nature is, by the standards of the Christian debate about original sin, very thin. At the centre of his vision is the functional, not the dysfunctional, family, but, it might be asked, is not the latter more the norm? Does he allow sufficiently for the degree to which the whole of society is caught up in various pathologies? Is this not the reason for the existence of people who are shameless and remorseless, invulnerable to any kind of shaming? And punishment, surely, does not appeal to people as rational actors but much more to a whole mesh of rather disreputable emotions, including vengeance, and the kind of sublimated masochism of Simone Weil's 'need for punishment'. Furthermore, as I noted in Chapter 5, we remain a hypocritical and a shaming society, and the way in which shaming processes work, through the media, is deeply stigmatizing and feeds a kind of moral schizophrenia with the 'page-three girl' on the next page to the denunciation of the 'sex fiend'.

For all these reasons we can hardly take the theory off the shelf as the answer to our needs. What Braithwaite does, however, is first to contextualize the whole justice debate in the wider question of society, where it certainly belongs, and then to make a profoundly important distinction between two kinds of shaming. In doing so he invites us to reflect upon our moral norms, and their enforcement, and to learn a way of expressing disapproval which does not stigmatize.

Mediation

Restorative justice works though mediation and reparation. I shall consider these practices in turn. Mediation has been defined as the intervention of a third party to help two or more parties in conflict to communicate and resolve their differences and achieve a settlement (consider this definition in relation to Ephesians 2.16 for example). It brings victim and offender face to face. If crime is fundamentally a matter of a broken relationship mediation is a means of repairing that relationship. This means that communication is at the heart of it. We know that offenders commonly neutralize their crime, arguing that it was trivial, or that the victim could afford it, or 'had it coming to them', or that it was not their fault. They also tend to see themselves as victims. This is much more difficult when they meet their victims. Offenders have repeatedly said that facing their victim is far harder than facing a court. Victim–offender encounters address the lack of respect which is the heart of the victim's experience of crime. For the victim, on the other hand, there is an opportunity to address fears and anger and to realize that the feared victimizer is weak and often helpless, evoking more pity than fear, more compassion than anger. Mediation destroys stereotypes on both sides, which in turn makes reconciliation possible.

Mediation can be regarded as retributive in the sense that it aims to induce the suffering of remorse in the offender. It clears the ground for reparation. In Braithwaite's terms it is reintegrative because, in bringing victim and offender together, it does not exclude but includes. Again, community is at the heart of the perception recognizing that offences cannot be dealt with by scapegoating, thrusting offenders *outside* the community, into jail, but can only be dealt with *within* the community. A model of this in action was the so-called 'hot seat' in Barlinnie jail in Scotland, used to try and reintegrate violent offenders. Jimmy Boyle, once dubbed 'the most violent man in Britain', and now a noted sculptor, was part of a small group on Christian name terms where differences were resolved by putting anyone committing an anti-social act in the 'hot seat' where they had to explain the reason for their actions. Boyle wrote:

> The key to the whole thing lies in the relationship of the people with the group, and the understanding that no one person is bigger than the community, that the commitment is to the community, and not the individual . . . I've experienced all sorts of punishments in my life and all have been very easy in comparison with the community hot seat. (Boyle, 1977, p. 252)

The practice of mediation rests on a recognition that conflict is normal rather than abnormal. It allows conflict to happen safely. The hot-seat procedure, which represents a form of mediation process, allows disputants to confront each other in a controlled setting. In Britain in the summer of 2003 we had a tragic story of two neighbours who had been arguing for years over a hedge. One shot and killed the other, and then, when arrested, committed suicide. The issue was trivial, but had generated intense conflict which ended in two deaths. It was a prime case for mediation.

The process implies a different view of law. If law, conventionally conceived, is a set of norms by which we evaluate cases, mediation is a process in which the norms are negotiated. It is a fundamental working out, between victim and offender, of what counts as moral behaviour and why. In this way law is de-professionalized and the participants in the process empowered. Mediators have no authority and do not pronounce a judgement. The parties concerned have to find the solution for themselves. Mediation processes highlight the inner drama of moral reflection. By contrast, the outer drama of the courtroom stigmatizes and alienates. Mediation also gives victims a chance to extend forgiveness, which allows them to put a closure to the whole experience.

Where victim–offender reconciliation programmes have been tried they have elicited high rates of satisfaction and have been shown to reduce recidivism rates. In Austria, virtually all juveniles accept the offer of mediation: 86 per cent of adult offenders accept it, and 84 per cent of victims; agreement is reached in 90 per cent of juvenile cases and 70 per cent of adult ones. Only 5 per cent proceed to a trial and 2 per cent to a conviction. In New Zealand, victims attend about half of family group conferences, in Australia somewhat more. In Britain, however, victim participation in restorative schemes remains low. In 2000–2001 less than 7 per cent of panels were attended by victims at youth offender panels. The Home Secretary's call, in summer 2003, for greater emphasis on such schemes is therefore extremely welcome.

As always we have to remind ourselves that such processes are not the promised land of criminal justice. Perhaps they are inappropriate for violent or hardened criminals, or for situations where one party has more administrative or economic power or personal dominance than the other. In relation to domestic violence some have objected that mediation processes do not give a strong enough message that domestic abuse is criminal. In the case of racial abuse it is questionable whether mediation can deal with politically motivated persecution, and it might not work in disputes involving large companies or a local authority. Again, some have expressed a fear that mediation might be marginalized by the criminal justice system if it refers only minor cases to the project or uses it as a dumping ground for those that are difficult but not serious. On the other hand, if we look at the huge number of cases of common assault which come before the courts (nearly 2 million in Britain in 2000), and the huge number of burglaries (more than 1 million), one cannot help thinking that making mediation the normal way of dealing with offenders would be both cost-effective and do something about changing the 'us and them', 'war against crime' culture in which we live.

Since reconciliation is so central a part of the gospel the churches ought to be enthusiastic supporters of such programmes. That they are not, and scarcely know what it is about, is bound up with the atrophying of confession, the loss of the sense of mutual accountability, the lack of practical experience of forgiveness in church communities. Tragically, church communities are identified by the wider community not as communities of forgiveness, which know how to deal with offences, but as moralizing and judgemental, repositories of excluding and reactionary attitudes (on areas to do with sexuality in particular). The practice of mediation, therefore, can be understood as a call to the churches to relearn their central gospel.

Reparation

As we saw in the last chapter, satisfaction, the idea of settling the differences between victim and offender by the making of compensation, was a standard part of earlier justice procedures and indeed some criminologists argue that it has been the main way of dealing with offences throughout history. It has been steadily revived over the past fifty years. Like mediation it gives a much larger place to the victim than the standard procedures of retributive justice. It shifts the focus from the offender's culpability to the harm suffered by the victim. It is far less costly than imprisonment and encourages offenders towards reintegration. The process of making reparation itself contributes to the rehabilitative process. At its heart is the concern that the offender takes responsibility for his or her action. Like mediation its aim is reconciliation between victim and offender. To some extent it is a symbolic process by which the offender does what is necessary (*satis facit*) to be included once more in the community. The Dutch criminologist Willem de Haan wants to make redress the centre of dealing with offending. Redress means to set right, put in good order again, remedy or remove trouble. To seek redress is to assert that an undesirable event has happened and that something needs to be done about it. It leaves open the way in which that ought to happen (de Haan, 1990).

Like mediation, reparation has a retributive element in that it is based on the assumption that harm done requires amends in the form of constructive action either for the victim or for their community. The community aspect is important, for reparation should not be understood simply as a transaction between victim and offender. The victim of an offence stands for the whole community which is damaged by crime. There is a context and, to use the debt metaphor for crime, it allows the offender to 'give something back to society'. At the same time the various treatment programmes involved in reparation may allow the community to make reparation to those offenders who have started life under handicaps. Thus, the means by which amends can be made include direct reparation, community service, but also such things as attending a drug treatment or alcohol treatment programme, or even undergoing plastic surgery and taking speech therapy to overcome self-image problems.

Justice as forgiveness

Mediation and reparation, when successful, issue in forgiveness. In terms of criminal justice this is problematic because states and courts cannot forgive, but only victims. Forgiveness as such cannot be part of the criminal justice system. On the other hand what we can have is a less adversarial legal culture which seeks to facilitate reconciliation and so forgiveness. This is the aspiration of restorative justice.

The recurring suspicion of forgiveness is that it means people get off 'scot free'. As I have noted in relation to mediation and reparation, both have their retributive aspects, as indeed does shaming. Forgiveness does not mean condoning crime. On the contrary, restorative justice, like retributive justice, insists that guilty acts are intrinsically worthy of punishment, reaffirms social norms, recognizes that the individual has a debt to society as a whole, and thus opens the way to reformation.

As noted in the previous chapter, the question of forgiveness applies differently to different types of crime. If I damage your car I pay for the damage, but do not need to beg for forgiveness, though characteristically my first words will be 'Sorry!' Forgiveness seems most obviously relevant in crimes against the person. In Britain some years ago newspapers reported that a vicar's daughter who had been subjected to a horrific rape in her own bedroom 'forgave the rapist'. The story carried a picture of the two sitting face to face. Behind the story is a process over many years in which she has struggled to come to terms with what happened to her, remake her life, and found that facing her attacker, now in jail, has been necessary to that process. Her forgiveness has not lessened his sentence, nor does it amount to a condoning of the crime, but it may help to heal him of whatever inner demons led to the attack. The long process involved seems essential. Another much more recent story involved the murder of two elderly people. At a press conference the day after the bodies were discovered, their children, both middle-aged, announced that they were Christians and so 'forgave the killers'. Something in us resists such easy forgiveness. It smacks of what Bonhoeffer called 'cheap grace'. Forgiveness, we want to say, is costly. It involves a struggle with grief, loss and anger. It is the overcoming of these things. 'Father, forgive them. They do not know what they are doing' is one thing as the cry of a dying man. It is another thing as an automatic reflex. Christian faith cannot mean that it should be that. At the same time it is true that forgiveness is not conditional. It is, rather, a form of prevenient grace. In the Gospels the story of Zacchaeus, the crooked tax-collector who systematically defrauded people for a lifetime and accrued a fortune in doing so, is a story of acceptance rather than forgiveness (for Jesus is not one of his victims, except insofar as he is a member of the tax-paying public) but it illustrates the way in which forgiveness works. It is by his acceptance that Jesus enables Zacchaeus' penitence, that he enables him to address his past and to 'become a new person', which is to say change his behaviour in the future. This is how forgiveness works.

Like every aspect of restorative justice, the practice of forgiveness can only be learned in community. Since forgiveness only works 'face to face' that may sound odd, until we return to our discussion of justice and the insistence that justice is a virtue which is only learned in community and that without the virtue of justice in individuals there can be no justice in community. Just so with forgiveness. To use the most overburdened word in the language, forgiveness presupposes love. Only love can forgive because only love is fully receptive to who somebody is. This brings us back to Braithwaite's communitarianism. Perhaps, like third-way politics, that is now dead in the water. What we cannot lose sight of is the social and political reality behind the slogan, which is the vision of a society where people really know and respond to one another, a community which does not operate by exclusion, which recognizes that there are less and more truly human ways of dealing with people, that seeks better practices of dealing with violence, of dealing with crime, and which is therefore passionately committed to social justice. At the root of restorative justice, in other words, is a community committed to shalom. One way of understanding Church is as a community which has that gospel as its remit. It is the Church, not particular loving individuals, which is a 'house of refuge', which offers a different social space to offenders. This is my theme in the final chapter.

9 | **The Church and the Prison**

The Christian community is to be found in the midst of the civil community. Though they are not the same they share the same centre and, although only a minority of the civil community are part of the Church, every Christian is a member of the civil community. The centre which they share is the rule of God, acknowledged in one case, unacknowledged in the other. The civil community is a secular community, embracing possibly many faith communities and, in contemporary Britain at least, a great many who are either agnostic or atheist. This does not mean that it has no theological significance. Isaiah believed Cyrus, King of Persia, was an instrument of God's will. Protestant thought has suggested, very differently from Augustine, that the civil community, or the state, may be regarded as a correspondence and analogue of God's kingdom. The civil community will sometimes be apostate. It will always leave much to be desired. However, when the affairs of the civil community are conducted in good faith, its concern will be the promotion of everything that furthers fullness of life, of shalom. Its understanding of fullness of life will differ greatly from that of the Christian community but there will be analogies. By the same token the Church is not concerned simply with 'spiritual' issues, with the next world. It is, as we have argued all along, concerned with the realization of shalom here and now. Politics is part of its brief. As part of its prophetic function it bears witness to what it believes to be God's will, as this is discerned from Scripture and in the light of tradition, and calls for the realization of that will in the civil community. In a pluralist society it is one voice among many seeking to make itself heard. It may be a voice which is small to vanishing but, unless it is heard in some way or other, the Church is untrue to its vocation. It is part of the civil community, and it addresses the civil community. That community, I have already insisted, includes those in prison. The prisoner forfeits his or her freedom, but does not cease to be a member of society. To some extent, as we have seen, society made him or her what they are.

The community and the prison

The mandate to visit prisons has always been honoured by some Christians. One of the problems with the growth of the prison as the main way of dealing with offenders was that the task of prison visiting quickly became professionalized. In the old unreformed prisons which Howard and Fielding documented, all sorts of people went in and out all the time. Gambling and prostitution were rife and there was a revolving door between crime inside and out. This meant that at the same time Christians exercising their mandate were also free to come and go. As the prison system grew this became far more difficult and responsibility was increasingly devolved on to chaplains who did the job on behalf of the community at large. There are two problems with this move.

First, there is a problem arising from the institutional position of the chaplain. The word 'chaplain' comes from the Latin *capella*, cloak. The chaplain was originally the cloak-bearer to a lord or high official; then he became a priestly assistant to a bishop; finally to guilds or institutions. By the sixteenth century chaplains were attached to armies and it was a natural extension of this to attach them to prisons, hospitals and other institutions.

The origin of the term 'chaplain', then, carries with it the implication that the chaplain is there to serve the establishment. In the armed forces the chaplains are officers. The worker-priest movement, which was influential in the 1950s, was suspicious of industrial chaplaincy because chaplains were seen as a tool of management. In prisons the chaplain was at one time second only to the governor. All chaplaincy suffers from the ambiguity that endorsement by 'the powers that be' confers. At the heart of the gospel is crucifixion by the powers. Is it possible for the Church to be employed by them? Does it not represent a necessary constraint on Christian freedom? In the prison the chaplain might only assist in institutionalizing the prisoners instead of performing his or her primary function of being a minister of the gospel. Even in the nineteenth century, it has been alleged, chaplains sometimes served a merely ornamental purpose, sitting with the governor on adjudications to provide some dignity and solemnity to what was taking place. Their sermons were tailored to suit bureaucratic interests. Religious teachings would not be allowed to stimulate sentiments that might subvert order and discipline. The church service might become just another perfunctory task the chaplain had to perform. A report on prison chaplaincy in Britain in 1919 noted that 'both chaplain and criminals were hard-hearted, and no-one, especially the chaplain, refrained from displaying boredom at the whole business . . . the outstanding features of the services were the cold mechanical method with which they ran themselves out and the obvious boredom of every-body concerned'.

A different kind of difficulty comes to the fore as society becomes more secularized after the 1960s. Up to the end of the previous decade, when conscription was still in force, recruits were asked on joining, 'Religion?' The answer 'Don't know' meant 'C of E' was written against their name. Despite some evidence that people continue to believe even when they do not belong it is clear that the currents of secularism run deep. Many people are avowedly secular and find clergy either irrelevant or offensive. The rise of counselling as a form of treatment means that after disasters or tragic events secular counsellors, rather than clergy, are now wheeled in. Chaplaincy rested on an acceptance of a shared Christian culture. It assumed that the great majority of people would want the offices of a minister for the rites of passage. This is increasingly not the case. The recognition of our multicultural society has led to the appointment of chaplains for other faith communities, but the deeper question is whether it is right for the state to pay ministers of any religion to provide services which the majority, when they have the freedom, have no interest in seeking. This is not to deny that chaplains often do a very important job, and especially in prison. Perhaps it is here above all that the difference between what the counsellor and what the priest or minister has to offer is felt. But we can put the question more sharply in another way: the job of the Christian (and not just ordained Christians or chaplains) is to preach the gospel. It is not a question of offering specifically spiritual help or advice to people, but of meeting them with the judgement and the claim of Jesus Christ. Could we expect the state to pay for that to be done?

The second problem with chaplains is that they do a job which properly belongs to the Christian community as a whole. At the Lincoln Conference on the theme of 'Respect in Prison' held in 1991, the Canadian prison chaplain Pierre Allard had this to say:

After 19 years as a prison chaplain (15 of these spent in a maximum security prison) my deepest conviction is that the community of crime must be impacted, not by individual chaplains, volunteers or other staff, but by the community of faith if truly the Good News is to become incarnate. In terms of the debate about penality, the walls of the prison should once again become permeable so that prisoners should be encouraged to become involved in the activities of the community and the community can take part in many of the activities of the prison.

My main purpose in this chapter is to endorse and underline this statement, and to consider its implications for the task of the Church. In order not to be misunderstood let me reiterate my conviction that many chaplains do a splendid job, and do it in the exercise of a particular charism which many other members of the Christian community may lack. Acknowledging the variety of gifts in the community is vital for the health of the Church. At the same time I think Allard is right for two reasons. First, because only a real recognition of the permeability of prison walls will enable society as a whole to accept that the prison is part of the wider community. Second, because the Church cannot in principle delegate its priestly, prophetic and diaconal functions to a few specialists. The chaplain is in jail on behalf of the Christian community, as its representative. This is good, but what is better is that the gifts of the body be available to that part of the community in prison as they are available to those outside. Every member of a Christian community will at once think of diverse gifts which all sorts of members of their community can make available to those in prison. Why should prisoners be denied that richness? It is bad for the Church and bad for those in prison. I begin, then, from the assumption that the Church, and not just 'the chaplain', belongs in prison. In this context the first task of the prison chaplain is to be an educator of the faith community, to help the faith community overcome the fear and distrust which the civil community has in general for those in prison.

Prisons, as we saw, are classic scapegoating places, where the sins of society at large are blamed on a small group who are driven out and then forgotten about. The civil community not in jail is often fearful, suspicious and driven by moral panics and badly informed judgements about that part of it which is. Chaplains are members of three communities: of the faith community, the civil community and the prison community. Their task must be to mediate between these three. They are storytellers of the truth about jails. This is at once a huge task and a liberation. It is a huge task because, on Allard's experience, it takes five years to educate just one faith community about prisons, and think how many churches of all denominations there are around our jails. But it is a liberation because it means that the whole burden of bearing witness to the love of God to those in prison does not fall on either the chaplain or the chaplaincy team. We are speaking of the Christian community, of which the chaplain is a representative and to which he or she is a witness. It is this community which is the true minister to those in prison. Henceforth I shall talk about the minister of the gospel in prison. I do not just mean the chaplain, though he or she is also that, but every member of the Christian community who becomes involved in prison ministry. I understand that, in the British context at least, this person is likely to be a chaplain for some time to come. I believe, however, that this is *faute de mieux*, and that we should look forward to the time when the whole community can offer ministry, in the wider context of making prison walls permeable.

The minister of the gospel preaches the gospel, the good news of the kingdom. To speak thus is to invite misunderstanding, for the word 'preach' is one of the most negative in the language. 'Stop preaching at me' is a common reproach. Preaching the gospel does not mean going into cells, Bible in hand, and talking to people about Jesus. There are a number of reasons for this but it is principally to do with the respect for the person at the heart of the gospel. The gospel is always gracious invitation. It is gracious: not something rammed down people's throats, or used to bang them on the head with. And it is an invitation: something people need to respond to at their own pace and in their own way. Much of what passes for evangelism is the opposite of gracious and there is quite enough ungracious activity in prison without Christians adding to it. On the other hand, the invitation is there to be made. Preaching the gospel of the kingdom, by which I mean, sharing the reasons we find the Christian faith centrally important and compelling, is no infringement of anyone's 'autonomy', providing it is done graciously, with modesty, tact, humour and respect.

The minister of the gospel (i.e. any Christian) faces the paradox that people are punished by being deprived of their freedom, but freedom is at the heart of the gospel. The minister of the gospel stands for freedom. 'For freedom Christ has set us free,' says Paul (Gal 5.1). 'The law of the Spirit of life in Christ Jesus has set you free' (Rom 8.2). If you continue in my word, says Jesus in John, 'you are truly my disciples, and you will know the truth, and the truth will make you free' (Jn 8.32).

What does the gospel of freedom mean for the unfree? It cannot be a pure spiritualization: don't worry about being locked up, you're free in spirit. The prisoner can then say: 'That's all very well for you. You can walk out of this place when you want to.' But Paul, who was a prisoner, did mean a freedom which transcended prison bars, the kind of freedom that Gandhi and Mandela exemplified in their spells in prison. This freedom arises from what we call in today's jargon, centredness. We are centred when we have meaning and purpose in our lives, freedom to have relationships which are purposeful and loving. It is that freedom which the minister of the gospel is there to help people to find. How?

The medieval theologians spoke of the priest as *alter Christus*, another Christ, which the Reformation then applied to every Christian. Where this is important in prison is that the representative of the community has to be one person at least in whom love and hope can be encountered. Near the beginning of the twentieth century a prison chaplain wrote: 'Preaching a religion of brotherly love to convicts while you are treating them upon a basis of hatred is a discouraging performance.' A little later two prison reformers observed:

> All Christian services and all Christian teaching in prison strike one with a sense of futility because the whole atmosphere of the prison life is a denial of Christianity. The forgiveness and love of God etc., are meaningless terms to a man who has never known forgiveness and love from men and is in prison because men refused to give them to him.

Sir David Ramsbotham, when Chief Inspector of Prisons, noted: 'Some staff exhibit a cynicism for positive programmes with prisoners, oppose the need to change long-established work patterns, and continually challenge the legitimate authority of the Prison service.' In this context, what does encountering the love of Christ mean concretely in the day-to-day situation in prison? I will try and sketch it in four ways, under the headings of courtesy, judgement, hope and power.

In the Middle Ages courtesy was a virtue which was highly prized. In this century we have been concerned with stripping off veneers and getting down to the reality behind appearances. We appreciate straight-from-the-shoulder, no-nonsense talking and acting. Courtesy is a thing of the past, as we know to our cost from behaviour on the roads. But in society as a whole, but especially in jail, courtesy is a vital and practical expression of respect for the other. The prison governor Andrew Coyle says rightly that within the walls of the prison the veneer of politeness which covers most human relationships is stripped away to be replaced by a naked clarity which goes right to the heart of how each of us feels about our fellow human beings. The normal rules of society do not apply and behaviour which would be unthinkable in everyday life somehow becomes acceptable. But as Lord Woolf noted in his report on prison disturbances in Britain, it is obvious that if prisoners are treated like animals, sworn at, degraded and psychologically toyed with week after week, they in turn lose respect, not only for their tormentors but for society at large. The minister of the gospel is one person who is called on to show courtesy even to the most wretched and unlovable creature. In doing that he or she really acts as *alter Christus* and breaks the mould of objectifying, hard-man, cynical behaviour. Where there is a chaplain, this will have to be someone who does not and cannot conform to prison service culture insofar as this embodies disrespect.

Another way of putting this would be to say that the minister of the gospel extends to prisoners the fellowship of what Jesus constituted as a society of 'friends' (Jn 15.15). Friendship combines affection with respect. It is not blind to a person's faults but always looks to their good sides and cherishes that of value in them. It lacks the intensity of erotic relationships, and is not based on the simple given of family. For these reasons it is easier for friends to give 'space', to allow people to be moody, introverted or even downright disagreeable, in the confident expectation that these moods will pass, that it will be possible to say 'sorry' and simply get on with things. Friendship is a rare commodity but, as the Quakers rightly realized, it ought to be a constitutive virtue of the body called Church. In an address to prison chaplains Rowan Williams insisted that one of the key jobs of the minister of the gospel is to remind people that they cannot be defined by one act, say, theft, rape or murder, that people are complex and have different selves in different contexts. The friend sees these contexts, tries to see the person as a whole, indeed tries to see the person not 'the criminal' (Williams, 1994).

Second, the minister of the gospel is under orders not to judge: 'Judge not that ye be not judged,' says Jesus. Coyle notes several times the danger that prison staff come to regard themselves as better human beings than the prisoners in their charge and that this is reflected in the way they treat them. A Calvinist liturgy of the late sixteenth century, written for the return of an offender to the community, ran:

> We in the sin of this our brother accuse and condemn our own sins, in his fall we all lament and consider our sinful nature, also we shall join repentance, tears, and prayers with him and his, knowing that no flesh can be justified before God's presence, if judgement proceed without mercy . . . We all here present join our sins with your sin; we all repute and esteem your fall to be our own; we accuse ourselves no less than you; and now finally we join our prayers with yours, that we may obtain mercy, and that by the means of our Lord Jesus Christ.

Today the Iona Community liturgy likewise involves two moments of confession and absolution in which minister and congregation say in turn, 'Before God, with the people of God, I confess to my brokenness: to the ways I wound my life, the lives of others, and the life of the world', and are absolved by each other. What would it mean if this practice of confession were used in jail? It is a practical acknowledgement of the truth that we are all sinners.

In prison, as part of the judicial process, where a person is judged and perhaps condemned on the part of society, the minister of the gospel, as God's representative, does not judge, cannot throw the first or the last stone. Sir David Ramsbotham talks of the attitude of those who work in prison. Think of the attitude with which Christ encounters people in the gospel. The minister of the gospel encounters people, not as the scum of society, rightfully locked up, but as God sees them, as children called to repentance and amendment of life just as everybody else is. In doing so they enable people to attend to what it is they are really called to be, to the nature of desire, the reality of their vulnerability.

Third, hope, real hope for a different kind of future, is often in short supply in prison. The minister of the gospel has good hope for all. What it means to hope, says Karl Barth,

> is to count upon it quite unconditionally that Jesus Christ has risen for each and every one; that his word as the Word of reconciliation is spoken for them personally; that the same Holy Spirit who has been incomprehensibly strong enough to enlighten his or her own dark heart will perhaps find a little less trouble with them one day. (Barth, 1962, p. 918)

It is with that hope that the minister of the gospel encounters all those he or she comes across, and I shall return to this in the next section.

Fourth, at the heart of the gospel is a perception about power. Paul understood this perfectly. God's power is made perfect in weakness, he says. Power, of course, is all around us, part of the fabric of life, in families, in couples, in the workplace. But prisons, especially, involve the exercise of power. The young men who form such a large part of the prison population value power in the form of physical strength and daring. More important is all the psychological manipulation, the jockeying for power within prisons, the establishment of pecking orders, picking on prisoners who have committed particularly unpleasant offences, sex offenders and the like. Then there is the power exercised by prison officers, which can sometimes go drastically wrong, or the use of prisoner power by officers. This is part of the daily reality of prison life.

The minister of the gospel has something to contribute here. Like any Christian he or she has to speak truth to power. Like any Christian he or she has to be on the side of the weakest, the prisoner who gets bullied by everyone.

Michael Ignatieff described the nineteenth-century prison chaplain as the 'technician of guilt'. A whole way of understanding Christianity was to rack up feelings of guilt, and then come in to meet them with the offer of forgiveness. One experienced prison chaplain notes that the chaplaincy is the one department in the prison charged with challenging people about 'change of life'. Its task is to ask people to consider their lives. It is the unique function of the chaplaincy, he says, to call to repentance so that forgiveness can be conveyed to those who reach out in trust, so that change may take place. It is the chaplaincy privilege to proclaim the good news that the result of sin – death in all its forms – has been defeated.

My problem with this is twofold. It does not acknowledge the need for discernment, but seems to assume that everyone in prison is a malefactor, whereas they are not. Second, it does not sufficiently acknowledge that all of us are in the same boat. Those not in prison need to repent as much as those inside. The whole of society needs to repent, and it is part of the gospel to proclaim that. Of course people have to be challenged to change of life, but this applies to the good people in the suburbs under their Neighbourhood Watch signs quite as much as those in prison.

From the Christian perspective guilt is both necessary to our humanity and destructive of it. The ability to acknowledge that I have been wrong, that I have made mistakes, that I need to ask forgiveness, is a fundamental part of humanness, according to the gospel. In this, Christians differ markedly from those humanists for whom guilt is always a bad thing, to be conjured away by psychiatrists. Christians, by contrast, say that guilt without forgiveness is destructive. Here we can agree that prison ministry can offer a vital opportunity for acknowledging guilt, and for finding forgiveness. Howard Zehr (1990) notes that as a society we lack the rituals which acknowledge that the debt has been paid and the guilt has been ended. The Sunday service in prison is somewhere where we can use our imagination about this and as it happens the Iona Community, again, has some rich liturgies of healing which enable just this.

Those who are whole have no need of a physician, only those who are sick need one. Every minister of the gospel knows, but prison officers and governors may not necessarily know, that the gospel is addressed not only to prisoners but also to prison officers and governors. Andrew Coyle observes that the most important set of relationships in any prison is that between the prisoner and the first-line prison officer. Somehow the minister of the gospel has to infect *that* relationship with grace and hope – difficult when it involves the slamming of metal doors and the turning of keys the entire time. A prison chaplain comments that his job is to bring life and hope to *each part* of the prison system and help it to work properly. The task is to find ways of structuring that into what is already a very full regime in a society where religion is regarded as an optional extra only of interest to the pious.

Exclusion, inclusion and shalom

In Chapter 1, and as the epigraph of the book, I quoted Winston Churchill's famous remark that a society is to be judged by the way it treats its offenders. By that standard the societies of Britain and the United States, in the past three decades, have been tried and found wanting. The new retributivism amounts to the belief that nothing works but that society can find a safety valve for its frustrations by punishing offenders. Prisoners, in my experience, share the view that nothing works. They are as sceptical of rehabilitation as anyone. With some honourable exceptions Christians, still tediously preoccupied with sexual ethics, have had rather little to say to this situation, partly, I suspect, because they read the need to punish out of their Scriptures. In general Girard is right that the gospel abolished scapegoating and the Church reinvented it. An Augustinian understanding of original sin can also feed the belief that the best we can do is to punish and to deter. But from the Christian point of view the 'nothing works' dogma is impossible. It is unbelief, and therefore sin. It is theology without eschatology.

The claim of the gospel is that, both immediately and over the long term, love works. Immediately, ministry to those in prison has to continue, and only makes sense, on the understanding that those found there are not subhuman but share the same need for redemption as the rest of us, and can indeed be redeemed. As Helen Prejean's *Dead Man Walking* illustrates so movingly, respect and acceptance 'work' even for those who have committed savage crimes. In the long term we come back to the need for hope in prison. Although our understanding of eschatology as a theology of hope is relatively recent, after the cultural collapse of the past three decades we find we have now to recover it. In this period hope has once again given way to 'realism', and there is a rejection of anything even vaguely utopian as it is assumed that utopias generally lead to terror, or at least to greater social control. But, as Moltmann argued, if hope is grounded in the resurrection, it is unable to put up with reality as it is (Moltmann, 1967). Hope is only utopian in believing in that which has no place *as yet*; it takes seriously the possibilities with which all reality is fraught, including that of the offender. The 'nothing works' dogma, masquerading as 'realism', is the opposite of resurrection hope. It is either resignation or despair. Because it believes that Christ is risen, hope insists on the possibilities of shalom, it insists that God rules and that God's rule has effects. How can we read the prophets, or the letter to the Romans, and forget that? That some utopian dreams ended in dystopia is not a reason for abandoning hope, but more a call to scrutinize what the grounds of hope are. The critique of Enlightenment, first articulated by Adorno and Horkheimer, precisely focused on the problem of vesting too much faith in the power of reason and forgot that reason without virtue was destructive (though critics from Goethe to Mary Shelley pointed this out at the time). 'Nothing works' pessimism both underestimates what has in fact been achieved, which is considerable, and trades on the nihilism of late capitalism, a negative apocalyptic which is content to see the world burn if profits can be made in the meantime. Shalom, as I have argued, has partial, very imperfect, but nevertheless worthwhile realizations in the provision of universal education and health care, in the provision of democratic freedoms and even, in places, in the care of offenders.

It is a fundamental characteristic of shalom that it is inclusive, not exclusive. Stanley Cohen rightly challenges us to face the difficulties involved in inclusion. It can fail to address issues of guilt and wrongdoing; it can lead to policies which inadvertently lead to the new forms of exclusion; and it can fail to address the real facts of human diversity (Cohen, 1985, p. 268). Liberal rhetoric always runs the risk of not facing real social difficulties, of being unimplementable. To avoid precisely such difficulties Reinhold Niebuhr opted for what he called 'Christian realism' but this in turn seemed only too often to sprinkle holy water on the status quo. Against such false realism we have to set the realism of hope. If such hope exists it is hope for the entire community and not just for a handful of brands plucked from the burning. This is the case because, as David Jenkins liked to say, it follows from our understanding of original sin that we can only be fully human if everyone is fully human. I acknowledged in the previous chapter that some communitarian thinking takes too idealistic a view of earlier communities. If we begin from the New Testament, rather than from Tönnies and Durkheim, we will want to say that fashioning community is an unfinished task (a task only to be completed in the kingdom). If Girard is right, and Christ abolishes the scapegoat principle, this community cannot be exclusive. This is not to say that some people should not be locked up. On the contrary, there are certainly people from whom society needs protecting (advertising moguls and military hardliners come to mind). What it is to say is that if people are locked up they are nevertheless recognized and treated *as those who continue to belong to society*, as those produced by society, and therefore as those *to whom society also continues to recognize a debt*. This necessarily entails ruling out the death penalty, which is the ultimate form of scapegoat penalty, the ultimate form of exclusion, and which breeds a violent and exclusionary culture within any society which practises it.

Penal policy in both Britain and the United States for more than twenty years has been committed to exclusion: to 'banging up' more and more prisoners, so that we have had to return to the prison ships of the early nineteenth century, and also to the private jails which John Howard warned were always a disaster in dealing with prisoners. Those responsible for 'justice' (i.e. scapegoating the poor) in Britain, Home Secretaries, to a man play to the gallery of the tabloid press, exploiting moral panics and depicting certain individuals or groups (in Britain it is currently paedophiles) as uniquely vicious. Of course I have no brief for paedophilia. I do, however, want to escape the stench of scapegoating about these political pronouncements, and to see some recognition of the fact that we are all responsible for the community we live in, which includes, unfortunately, child murderers and paedophiles, just as it includes dictators immune from prosecution who are responsible for the torture of thousands, or World Bank officials who urge dumping toxic waste in developing countries. We are all members one of another: that is the bottom line of penal policy, and it precludes scapegoating. The question we are up against in framing criminal justice policy is not 'containing' or 'dealing with' crime. It is the question of what humans are on the way to becoming and how we can work together to improve our chances of becoming better. In relation to criminal justice this means two things. First, it means that, while there will always be a need for some imprisonment (though not at present levels) prisons should exist in vigorous interaction with their surrounding communities. Second, that social conditions are not fate and that we can do things to improve social justice. The criminal justice system will only be morally defensible when a far greater degree of practical equality than exists at present has been established. In this respect Paul's famous pronouncement that 'in Christ' there can be no ethnic, gender or class boundaries is a description of the Church's task in an alienated society. It is not simply a description of the kingdom of God beyond this world. Church exists to witness to the reconciling work of the God of peace, overcoming alienation here and now, and therefore (since no man is an island) reconstituting society. Unlike the optimistic Christian socialists of the first part of the twentieth century we know that we cannot 'bring in' the kingdom, but on the other hand we look for the realization of small concrete utopias, situations of shalom which are much less unjust than what we currently have. This applies to criminal justice as to all other areas of life. Shalom, the peace and justice of God, is both the context and the goal of criminal justice. Without justice, asked Augustine, what are kingdoms but bands of robbers? Let me rephrase that: without shalom as our norm and goal what is justice but the rule of the strong, and what is the rule of the strong but violence? Micah asked for justice to run down like waters. The justice he had in mind was an inclusionary justice, based on peace and equity. It is the fundamental framework for the Church's understanding of crime.

Suggestions for Further Reading

Chapter 1: Shalom

The best discussion of shalom, and of the biblical account of justice, known to me is U. Duchrow and G. Liedke, *Shalom: Biblical Perspectives on Creation, Peace and Justice* (Geneva: World Council of Churches, 1987). Jürgen Moltmann's *The Way of Jesus Christ* (London: SCM Press, 1990) also has some helpful remarks on the gospel of peace. Stanley Cohen's *Visions of Social Control* (Cambridge: Polity, 1985), Jock Young's *The Exclusive Society* (London: Sage, 1999) and David Garland's *The Culture of Control* (Oxford: Oxford University Press, 2001) all offer illuminating analyses of the present situation in criminal justice in Britain and the United States. Throughout I have drawn on Karl Barth's political writings, published as *Against the Stream* (London: SCM Press, 1954) as also on the *Church Dogmatics*, and especially vol. IV.3 (Edinburgh: T & T Clark, 1962).

Chapter 2: Law and the Life of the Community

Thomas Aquinas' discussion of law can be found in vol. 28 of the New Blackfriars edition of *Summa Theologiae* (*ST*). There is a helpful discussion of the Reformation position in J. Witte, *Law and Protestantism: The Legal Teachings of the Lutheran Reformation* (Cambridge: Cambridge University Press, 2002). Durkheim's illuminating discussion of crime and law can be found in *The Division of Labour in Society* (London: Macmillan, 1984). H. A. L. Hart, *The Concept of Law* (Oxford: Clarendon Press, 1961) is still fundamental but needs to be read alongside critiques such as P. Fitzpatrick, *The Mythology of Modern Law* (London: Routledge, 1992). Ronald Dworkin's work can be found in *Taking Rights Seriously* (London: Duckworth, 1978) and *Law's Empire* (London: Fontana, 1986). This, too, needs to be read alongside critique, for example in V. Kerruish, *Jurisprudence as Ideology* (London: Routledge, 1991). John Finnis represents a continuation of the natural law tradition in *Natural Law and Natural Rights* (Oxford: Clarendon Press, 1980). There are excellent editions of Cicero's *On the Laws* and *On Duties*, of Montesquieu's *The Spirit of the Laws* and Beccaria's *On Crimes and Punishments* in the Cambridge Political Texts series. U. Duchrow, *Global Economy: A Confessional Issue for the Churches?* (Geneva: World Council of Churches, 1987) offers an abbreviated version of his earlier far-ranging discussion of the Lutheran two-kingdoms theory which is only available in German.

Chapter 3: Social Justice and Criminal Justice

The texts of Plato and Aristotle are available in many translations but I have used the collections of Hamilton and Cairns (Princeton, 1961) for Plato and of J. Barnes (Oxford, 1985) for Aristotle. C. Marshall offers a wide-ranging reflection on the New Testament understanding of criminal justice in *Beyond Retribution: A New Testament Vision for Justice, Crime and Punishment* (Grand Rapids: Eerdmans, 2001). Aquinas' reflections on justice can be found in *ST*, vol. 37 of the New Blackfriars edition. E. C. Gardner offers a somewhat partial account of the Protestant tradition in *Justice and Christian Ethics* (Cambridge: Cambridge University Press, 1995); J. Rawls, *A Theory of Justice* (Oxford: Oxford University Press, 1973) is a modern classic. There is excellent discussion of this and of the whole range of issues in this chapter in D. Forrester, *Christian Justice and Public Policy* (Cambridge: Cambridge University Press, 1997). D. Miller, *Social Justice* (Oxford: Oxford University Press, 1976), also includes an interesting discussion of Rawls. J. Shklar offers an excellent polemical statement of the Platonic tradition in *The Faces of Injustice* (New Haven: Yale, 1990). B. Hudson's *Penal Policy and Social Justice* (London: Macmillan, 1993) is also helpful.

Chapter 4: Crime and Responsibility

The Oxford Handbook of Criminology (3rd edn), edited by R. Maguire *et al.* (Oxford: Oxford University Press, 2002), offers a quite outstanding series of essays on most areas of the topic of crime. Also worth consulting are S. Cote (ed.), *Criminological Theories* (London: Sage, 2002), Fitzgerald *et al.*, *Crime and Society* (London: Routledge, 1981), and I. Taylor, P. Walton and J. Young, *The New Criminology*

(London: Routledge, 1973) – not new any longer, but eloquent testimony to a less disenchanted world. On white-collar crime I have found G. Slapper and S. Tombs, *Corporate Crime* (London: Longman, 1999) exceptionally helpful; also M. Clinard and P. Yeager, *Corporate Crime* (New York: Free Press, 1980), S. Box, *Power, Crime and Mystification* (London: Tavistock, 1983), J. Braithwaite, *Corporate Crime in the Pharmaceutical Industry* (London: Routledge, 1984), and G. Slapper, *Blood in the Bank* (Aldershot: Ashgate, 1999). On sin, A. McFadyen's discussion in *Bound to Sin* (Cambridge: Cambridge University Press, 2000) is illuminating, as is Barth's discussion of pride, sloth and the lie in vol. 4 of the *Church Dogmatics*.

Chapter 5: Paying the Price

The literature on punishment is vast. Among the best discussions are W. Moberly, *The Ethics of Punishment* (London: Faber, 1968), E. Moberly, *Suffering, Innocent and Guilty* (London: Darton, Longman & Todd, 1978), B. Hudson, *Justice through Punishment* (London: Macmillan, 1987), D. Garland, *Punishment and Modern Society* (Oxford: Clarendon Press, 1990), R. Duff, *Trials and Punishments* (Cambridge: Cambridge University Press, 1986), and R. Duff and D. Garland's *A Reader on Punishment* (Oxford: Oxford University Press, 1994). From this Reader I have cited especially H. Bianchi, 'Abolition: assensus or sanctuary'. J. Braithwaite and P. Pettit's *Not Just Deserts* (Oxford: Clarendon Press, 1990) is an argument for decrements in punishment which almost persuades one that consequentialism is respectable. I have also used S. Weil, *The Need for Roots* (London: Routledge, 1987). G. B. Shaw's impassioned polemic in S. and B. Webb, *English Prisons Under Local Government* (London: Longman, 1922) is well worth consulting. H. Parker *et al.*, *Unmasking the Magistrates* (Milton Keynes: Open University, 1989) offers some rather chilling insights on what magistrates think they are doing in sentencing. My own *God's Just Vengeance* (Cambridge: Cambridge University Press, 1996) seeks to offer a theological reflection on the criminal justice process. Walter Wink's great trilogy on the Powers is never far from the discussion. Here I cite *Engaging the Powers* (Minneapolis: Fortress Press, 1992).

Chapter 6: Prison

M. Foucault, *Discipline and Punish* (Harmondsworth: Penguin, 1977) and M. Ignatieff, *A Just Measure of Pain* (Harmondsworth: Penguin, 1978) are both fundamental here. A. Coyle, *The Prisons We Deserve* (Glasgow: HarperCollins, 1994) is written by someone who is both a prison governor and a Christian. The Church of Scotland Report edited by C. Wood, *The End of Punishment* (Edinburgh: St Andrew Press, 1991), is also excellent. Accounts by prisoners such as J. Boyle, *A Sense of Freedom* (Edinburgh: Canongate, 1977) are helpful. Lord Woolf's report on the prison disturbances in Manchester in 1990 is an illuminating document, though arguably out of date (London: HMSO, 1991). T. Mathiesen's *Prison on Trial* (Winchester: Waterside, 2000) is one of the most respected calls for abolition.

Chapter 7: Victims and Offenders

The essays in L. Lampmann and M. Shattuck (eds), *God and the Victim* (Grand Rapids: Eerdmans, 1999) vary enormously in quality but those by M. Volf and N. Wolterstorff are especially good. The same goes for R. Davis *et al.* (eds), *Victims of Crime* (London: Sage, 1997) where the best essay is by E. Fattah whose *Towards a Critical Victimology* (London: Macmillan, 1992) is one of the best texts on the subject. R. Mawby and S. Walklate, *Critical Victimology* (London: Sage, 1994) can also be consulted. P. Trible, *Texts of Terror* (Philadelphia: Fortress Press, 1984) is a justly celebrated, though disturbing, set of exegeses of stories of women victims in the Old Testament. R. Williams, *Resurrection* (London: Darton, Longman & Todd, 1982) helps us to understand the resurrection in terms of forgiveness, and G. Jones, *Embodying Forgiveness* (Grand Rapids: Eerdmans, 1995) is a superb discussion of the topic.

Chapter 8: Justice and Reconciliation

Howard Zehr, *Changing Lenses* (Scottdale: Herald, 1990) is a foundational text for theological reflection on restorative justice. M. Wright, *Justice for Victims and Offenders* (Winchester: Waterside, 1996) offers a good survey of the ground, and J. Burnside and N. Baker, *Relational Justice* (Winchester: Waterside, 1994) offers many stimulating essays. J. Braithwaite's *Crime, Shame and Reintegration* (Cambridge: Cambridge University Press, 1989) has proved to be a seminal text. Also of interest is P. Howley's somewhat chaotically written *Breaking Spears and Mending Hearts* (London: Zed, 2002), an account of restorative justice processes in Papua New Guinea. W. de Haan, *The Politics of Redress* (London: Unwin Hyman, 1990) is an abolitionist manifesto which concentrates on the alternative.

Chapter 9: The Church and the Prison

I have drawn here on the closing chapters of J. Milbank's seminal work *Theology and Social Theory* (Oxford: Blackwell, 1990) and on J. Moltmann's even more seminal *Theology of Hope* (London: SCM Press, 1967).

Throughout I have found articles in the journal of the prison chaplaincy in England, *New Life*, extremely helpful. In particular I should mention P. Jennings, 'Going to prison' (vol. 4, 1987); R. Stokes, 'The changing chaplaincy' and B. Frost, 'Forgiveness and politics' (vol. 5, 1988); R. Williams, 'Penance in the penitentiary', H. Potter, 'Shades of the prison house' (vol. 7, 1990); H. Potter, 'Speaking from the heart' (vol. 8, 1991); S. Sykes, 'Beyond justice: building hope into our prisons' (vol. 10, 1993); R. Williams, 'Ministry in prison', D. Forrester, 'Relationships in prison' (vol. 11, 1994); and D. Lamplugh, 'Finding peace as a relative of a victim' (vol. 13, 1997). My thanks to Alan Duce for making these available. He also made available transcripts of conferences on prison chaplaincy which were likewise most useful, especially the papers by David Jenkins at the 1989 conference and by Howard Zehr, Pierre Allard and Brian Frost at the 1991 conference.

Select Bibliography

Barth, K., 1962. *Church Dogmatics*, Edinburgh: T & T Clark.

Bianchi, H., 1994. 'Abolition: assensus or sanctuary' in R. Duff and D. Garland, *A Reader on Punishment*, Oxford: Oxford University Press.

Box, S., 1983. *Power, Crime and Mystification*, London: Tavistock.

Boyle, J., 1977. *A Sense of Freedom*, Edinburgh: Canongate.

Braithwaite, J., 1984. *Corporate Crime in the Pharmaceutical Industry*, London: Routledge.

Braithwaite, J., 1989. *Crime, Shame and Reintegration*, Cambridge: Cambridge University Press.

Braithwaite, J. and Pettit, P., 1990. *Not Just Deserts*, Oxford: Clarendon Press.

Clinard, M. and Yeager, P., 1980. *Corporate Crime*, New York: Free Press.

Cohen, S., 1985. *Visions of Social Control*, Cambridge: Polity Press.

Coyle, A., 1994. *The Prisons We Deserve*, Glasgow: HarperCollins.

de Haan, W., 1990. *The Politics of Redress*, London: Unwin Hyman.

Duchrow, U., 1987. *Global Economy: A Confessional Issue for the Churches*, Geneva: World Council of Churches.

Duff, R., 1986. *Trials and Punishments*, Cambridge: Cambridge University Press.

Dworkin, R., 1978. *Taking Rights Seriously*, London: Duckworth.

Dworkin, R., 1986. *Law's Empire*, London: Fontana.

Fattah, E., 1997. Essay in R. Davis (ed.), *Victims of Crime*, London: Sage.

Fitzpatrick, P., 1992. *The Mythology of Modern Law*, London: Routledge.

Forrester, D., 1994. 'Relationships in prison', *New Life*, vol. 11.

Forrester, D., 1997. *Christian Justice and Public Policy*, Cambridge: Cambridge University Press.

Garland, D., 2001. *The Culture of Control*, Oxford: Oxford University Press.

Hart, H. A. L., 1961. *The Concept of Law*, Oxford: Clarendon Press.

Hayek, F., 1976. *The Mirage of Social Justice*, London: Routledge.

Hudson, B., 1993. *Penal Policy and Social Justice*, London: Macmillan.

Lamplugh, D., 1997. 'Finding peace as a relative of a victim', *New Life*, vol. 13.

Milbank, J., 1990. *Theology and Social Theory*, Oxford: Blackwell.

Miller, D., 1976. *Social Justice*, Oxford: Oxford University Press.

Moltmann, J., 1967. *Theology of Hope*, London: SCM Press.

Moltmann, J., 1990. *The Way of Jesus Christ*, London: SCM Press.

Parker, H. *et al.*, 1989. *Unmasking the Magistrates*, Milton Keynes: Open University.

Rawls, J., 1973. *A Theory of Justice*, Oxford: Oxford University Press.

The Report of the Commission on Social Justice, 1994. London: Vintage.

Shklar, J., 1990. *The Faces of Injustice*, New Haven: Yale.

Slapper, G., 1999. *Blood in the Bank*, Aldershot: Ashgate.

Slapper, G. and Tombs, S., 1999. *Corporate Crime*, London: Longman.

Taylor, I., Walton, P. and Young, J., 1973. *The New Criminology*, London: Routledge.

Trible, P., 1984. *Texts of Terror*, Philadelphia: Fortress Press.

Volf, M., 1999. Essay in L. Lampmann and M. Shattuck (eds), *God and the Victim*, Grand Rapids, Eerdmans.

Williams, R., 1982. *Resurrection*, London: Darton, Longman & Todd.

Williams, R., 1994. 'Ministry in prison', *New Life*, vol. 11.

Wink, W., 1992. *Engaging the Powers*, Minneapolis: Fortress Press.

Witte, J., 2002. *Law and Protestantism: The Legal Teachings of the Lutheran Reformation*, Cambridge: Cambridge University Press.

Wolterstorff, N., 1999. Essay in L. Lampmann and M. Shattuck (eds), *God and the Victim*, Grand Rapids, Eerdmans.

Young, J., 1999. *The Exclusive Society*, London: Sage.

Zehr, H., 1990. *Changing Lenses*, Scottdale: Herald.

Index

The Society for Promoting Christian Knowledge (SPCK) was founded in 1698. Its mission statement is:

To promote Christian knowledge by

- **Communicating the Christian faith in its rich diversity;**
- **Helping people to understand the Christian faith and to develop their personal faith; and**
- **Equipping Christians for mission and ministry.**

SPCK Worldwide serves the Church through Christian literature and communication projects in over 100 countries, and provides books for those training for ministry in many parts of the developing world. This worldwide service depends upon the generosity of others and all gifts are spent wholly on ministry programmes, without deductions.

SPCK Bookshops support the life of the Christian community by making available a full range of Christian literature and other resources, providing support for those training for ministry, and assisting bookstalls and book agents throughout the UK.

SPCK Publishing produces Christian books and resources, covering a wide range of inspirational, pastoral, practical and academic subjects. Authors are drawn from many different Christian traditions, and publications aim to meet the needs of a wide variety of readers in the UK and throughout the world.

The Society does not necessarily endorse the individual views contained in its publications, but hopes they stimulate readers to think about and further develop their Christian faith.

For further information about the Society, visit our website at
www.spck.org.uk, or write to:
SPCK, Holy Trinity Church, Marylebone Road,
London NW1 4DU, United Kingdom.